# TO TWILO AND BEYOND!

# TO TWILO AND BEYOND!

◆

## My Walnut Adventures with *The Dick Van Dyke Show* Cast

David Van Deusen

Preface by Carl Reiner

iUniverse, Inc.
New York  Lincoln  Shanghai

# TO TWILO AND BEYOND!
## My Walnut Adventures with *The Dick Van Dyke Show* Cast

Copyright © 2005 by David Van Deusen

All rights reserved. No part of this book may be used or reproduced by any means, graphic, electronic, or mechanical, including photocopying, recording, taping or by any information storage retrieval system without the written permission of the publisher except in the case of brief quotations embodied in critical articles and reviews.

iUniverse books may be ordered through booksellers or by contacting:

iUniverse
2021 Pine Lake Road, Suite 100
Lincoln, NE 68512
www.iuniverse.com
1-800-Authors (1-800-288-4677)

ISBN-13: 978-0-595-37380-2 (pbk)
ISBN-13: 978-0-595-81776-4 (ebk)
ISBN-10: 0-595-37380-1 (pbk)
ISBN-10: 0-595-81776-9 (ebk)

Printed in the United States of America

To my kids,
Amy, Dan, and Kelly,
Who love me in spite of my "nuttiness!"

# Contents

Preface . . . . . . . . . . . . . . . . . . . . . . . . . . . . . . . . . . . . . . . . . . . . . . . . ix
What the cast is saying… . . . . . . . . . . . . . . . . . . . . . . . . . . . . . . . . . xi

| | | |
|---|---|---|
| Chapter 1 | How It All Began. . . . . . . . . . . . . . . . . . . . . . . . . . 1 |
| Chapter 2 | Rose Marie . . . . . . . . . . . . . . . . . . . . . . . . . . . . . . 7 |
| Chapter 3 | Morey Amsterdam. . . . . . . . . . . . . . . . . . . . . . . . 21 |
| Chapter 4 | Ann Guilbert . . . . . . . . . . . . . . . . . . . . . . . . . . . 31 |
| Chapter 5 | Sheldon Leonard . . . . . . . . . . . . . . . . . . . . . . . . 39 |
| Chapter 6 | Earle Hagen. . . . . . . . . . . . . . . . . . . . . . . . . . . . 46 |
| Chapter 7 | Dick Van Dyke . . . . . . . . . . . . . . . . . . . . . . . . . 54 |
| Chapter 8 | Carl Reiner . . . . . . . . . . . . . . . . . . . . . . . . . . . . 69 |
| Chapter 9 | Mary Tyler Moore . . . . . . . . . . . . . . . . . . . . . . . 82 |
| Chapter 10 | Larry Mathews. . . . . . . . . . . . . . . . . . . . . . . . . . 90 |
| Chapter 11 | Behind the Camera . . . . . . . . . . . . . . . . . . . . . . 99 |
| Chapter 12 | Julie Paris, Bill Idelson, Frank Adamo and the other Guest Stars. . . . . . . . . . . . . . . . . . 118 |
| Chapter 13 | The Making of "It May Look Like a Walnut" . . 130 |
| Chapter 14 | Merchandise, TV Specials, and DVDs. . . . . . . . 142 |
| Chapter 15 | The TV LAND Awards. . . . . . . . . . . . . . . . . . 153 |
| Chapter 16 | *The Dick Van Dyke Show Revisited*. . . . . . . . . . . 165 |

**Chapter 17** The Final Chapter . . . . . . . . . . . . . . . . . . . . . . . 180
About the Author . . . . . . . . . . . . . . . . . . . . . . . . . . . . . . . . . 183

# *Preface*

Little did I know that *The Dick Van Dyke Show*, which had been a well received television series, would so pique the interest of a viewer, that he would one day publish a newsletter which he named, *The Walnut Times*—after one of my favorite episodes, "It May Look Like A Walnut." That intrepid and perceptive viewer had taken it upon himself to become the voluntary historian and archaeologist of the almost half-century-old *The Dick Van Dyke Show*—and all of us connected with the show could not be more pleased that he took on this task.

For the last ten years, I have enjoyed reading and being entertained by his quarterly publication and marveled at how he filled each copy with information, interviews and reminiscences. When David Van Deusen wrote and said that he was sending me a copy of this book and asked if I would write a preface for it, I hedged and said that I would not say yes until I read what he had written. Well, it is obvious that I liked what I read because here I am contributing a few words of honest praise for his work.

I read the book in one comfortable sitting and was absolutely amazed about the things he had discovered about the show and its personnel, and how much I had not known about the cast members and their experiences—both during that period of production and at the present time. By doggedly going about contacting everyone ever connected with *The Dick Van Dyke Show*, David Van Deusen has unearthed information and anecdotes about those good old days and the good, young actors and directors who made it work. He has given me a second look at things that I was too busy to look at the first time around and I thank him and his book for affording me that rare and pleasant opportunity.

Carl Reiner

# *What the cast is saying...*

As far as I know, nobody thought of keeping a diary during the unforgettable years of our show. As it turns out, it wasn't necessary. Reading his book, I would swear that David had been there every step of the way. It tweaked my memory in wonderful ways and I missed those days all over again. Thank you, David, for your loving commitment to our memory.

*Dick Van Dyke*

*To Twilo And Beyond* is filled with the personal experiences of us all as we worked together for five gloriously silly years. My "Mary Richard's" hat is off to David Van Deusen for an excellent return visit with family.

*Mary Tyler Moore*

For any fan of *The Dick Van Dyke Show*, this book is a MUST read. David has captured the soul of each character to a "T." You will not be able to put this book down until you finish reading it. Enjoy all the wonderful memories!

*Rose Marie*

Cheers to David Van Deusen for keeping the spirit of *The Dick Van Dyke Show* alive and well. Thanks to him, the world will be able to keep its love affair of *DVD* going forever. Who knows? Maybe the world will even be moved to remember a certain has-been ex child star!

*Larry Mathews*

Surely the most ardent fan of the *DVD Show* is that other DVD, Dave Van Deusen. He has kept me trodding down Memory (Bonnie Meadow) Lane for years.

*Ann Guilbert*

Maybe it was his initials that got David so interested in the *DVD Show*. We're glad he did. It's a wonderful book and we're so glad his last name isn't Flanagan.

*Sam Denoff*

Anyone who is fond of *The Dick Van Dyke Show* will enjoy *To Twilo and Beyond* by that other DVD—David Van Deusen.

*John Rich*

David Van Deusen's passion for *The Dick Van Dyke Show* is surpassed only by the sincere genuineness of the friendships that he has established with the entire *DVDS* family. His sharing of these experiences gives other fans a personal and unique look at this terrific cast.

*Julie Paris*

Several years ago I had the good fortune to be the film editor of *The Dick Van Dyke Show*. About a year ago, I had the good fortune of meeting David Van Deusen (aka the "Head Walnut"). And today, thanks to David's book, I can enjoy those marvelous memories again.

*Bud Molin*

I feel a little funny about offering any sentiment at all because I did so few shows and was such a minor player. But what the hell? I enjoyed the book very much!

*Bill Idelson*

The continued loyalty of *The Dick Van Dyke Show* is due in part to the publication of its fan club newsletter, *The Walnut Times*. The publisher and writer of this informative newsletter, David Van Deusen, keeps the current audience informed as to the performers and stars of the original cast.

*Earle Hagen*

# *Acknowledgements*

There are several people who must be acknowledged for their help, not only with the creation of this book, but also with the generous assistance provided to me in my publishing of *The Walnut Times*.

To Pat Schoof, my interview transcriptionist, who has spent countless hours transcribing celebrity interviews and typing them up into electronic format for me. Thanks Pat. I couldn't have done it without you!

To John Graziano, an absolutely fabulous artist, who is the individual responsible for nearly all of the fantastic artwork I have in the newsletter and in this book. This includes the newsletter logo and the title lettering of this book in *Dick Van Dyke Show* lettering, the great caricature of Dick Van Dyke shown on the back cover, the superb drawing of Dick, Rose Marie, and Morey on *The Walnut Times* t-shirt, the wonderful 40$^{th}$ Anniversary caricature print which I commissioned in 2001, and much more. John is currently the artist for the nationally syndicated *Ripley's Believe It or Not*! Thanks, John, for your generosity in sharing your amazing talents at such "reasonable" rates.

To Michael Wilhelm and Paul Idelson, two individuals who continually encouraged me to put my *Dick Van Dyke Show* stories down on paper, insisting that other fans would be genuinely interested in reading about them. I hope they're right! Michael is also a very talented artist in his own right and provided the artwork drawing of me, Carl, and Dick in Chapter One. Paul is the son of writer/producer Bill Idelson and made several beneficial suggestions about many aspects of the book. Thanks to both of you guys!

And finally, to Greg Williams, a native of Danville, Illinois, Dick's home town, who, believe it or not, lives on Walnut Street in Danville. Yes, *Walnut* Street! Is that a coincidence or what? Not only is Greg a loyal subscriber to the newsletter, most importantly for me, he is an English Department chairperson and teacher at Danville High School. After reading a couple of chapters of my manuscript, Greg selflessly volunteered to be the editor for my book—and what help he provided! He reviewed and edited the entire manuscript in a couple of week's time and gave very positive and constructive feedback. Thanks, Greg, for all of your assistance. I would not have a finished book without your aid and support!

# 1

## *How It All Began*

The title credits flash on the screen, and that familiar tune starts to play...the front door opens, and in steps Rob Petrie...a quick kiss for Laura and a quick step toward the living room...and then...whoop boom!! Down Rob tumbles in that classic "trip" over the ottoman. This opening segment is probably one of the more recognized in television sitcom history...and that, of course, is *The Dick Van Dyke Show*.

I was just a year old when *The Dick Van Dyke Show* premiered on October 3, 1961, on CBS. And before I go any further, yes, I do have the same initials as Dick Van Dyke, and, no, I didn't change my name just so I could have the same initials as Dick—it is purely a coincidence. But it's a nice coincidence and a fun and unique connection at that! I am often asked that question and must admit that my name was of my parent's own doing (interestingly, my dad's name was Dick!). Enough about that!

In the early 1990s, I began to collect all of the 158 episodes of *The Dick Van Dyke Show* on videotape, one by one, taping them off of cable stations in my area which broadcast the show. I created a computer database to keep track of the episodes and updated it as new ones were captured along the way. At first, it was easy since I was starting from nothing, but as I began to fill out the collection, it became a little trickier and required some more intensive scrutiny of the TV schedules to nail down the remaining elusive episodes which I had yet to add to my collection.

As I continued in my quest to record all of the shows on tape, it afforded me the opportunity to watch virtually all of the shows and, at the same time, come to the realization of what an amazing show this really was! Even as a kid, I had always been entertained by the outstanding individual and stellar cast performances of *The Dick Van Dyke Show* ensemble of actors and actresses. And looking back at the shows now as an adult, I was able to gain a true appreciation for the cast's talents and the quality storylines which were created during the show's five year stint. Not only did the episode storylines contain situations to which I could easily relate, I especially appreciated the various skits, comedy, and musical numbers which were performed throughout the life of the show. What a talented group of people! I would assert that there has been none finer and more diversified since that time.

As I completed the final collection of episodes, I decided it would be a nice idea to write to the cast members and let them know how much their work from so many years ago was still being treasured today! I set out to the library to see if I could find addresses where I could contact the cast. While I was there, I also tried to find out if there was a *Dick Van Dyke Show* fan club of some kind. Nope. Certainly not anything that jumped out at me.

Then the thought occurred to me. What if I were to start a *Dick Van Dyke Show* fan club? What a nice gesture it would be to the cast from the show—a tip of the hat so to speak—to let them know in a more formal way how much their entertainment had been enjoyed years ago and was still being enjoyed today.

As I was sending out letters of appreciation to the cast, I also wrote to Viacom, the company responsible for airing the show in syndication, to ask if it would be possible to start a fan club for the show. The short answer? No! The long answer? Read on.

Citing that Viacom had recently signed a contract for merchandising rights to the show and that they were not sure if this might include a fan club, my request was denied. It was short and sweet and to the point—I could *not* start a fan club. And not only did I receive this letter, but a copy was also sent to Dick Van Dyke and Dick's attorney. It wasn't looking good.

Of course, I found it difficult to take "no" for an answer. As I began to receive autographed photos and positive correspondence back from the cast members in response to my letters of appreciation, I pondered what I might do to still recognize the cast's achievements and provide a way for fans of the show to demonstrate their appreciation of one of the classiest shows in television sitcom history.

I networked with other individuals who were currently running fan clubs to see what insights they might be able to offer me. I crossed paths with a gal by the name of Linda Kay, who was the leader of the National Association of Fan Clubs.

"Why don't you start a newsletter about the show," Linda suggested, "and give the publication a name that fans will recognize as being associated with *The Dick Van Dyke Show*. How about *Life in New Rochelle*?" She continued, "You have your First Amendment right to write about anything you would like to, so as long as you don't infringe on anyone's rights, you should be fine."

I liked Linda's idea about starting a publication and gave some serious consideration to the suggestion but thought I could come up with a better title. After all, if it was successful, the publication could be around for awhile and would need to have a memorable name. What should I call it? How would fans of the show be able to relate to my newsletter?

One of my favorite episodes from the show was the famous "It May Look Like a Walnut" segment—whether it was the mental image of Rob losing his thumbs or Laura sliding down the mountain of walnuts. After much deliberation, I decided to call the newsletter *The Walnut Times*. And it was not very long before I knew that I had a winner! The most typical question from potential subscribers was "Does this have something to do with the walnut episode?"

Logo and lettering by John Graziano

With title in hand, I sat down to establish the layout and content of the periodical. What should be included? How often should it be published? How many pages would it be?

I wanted to include cast interviews, if I could possibly make them happen, as well as rarely seen black & white and color photos from the show. The current day happenings of the cast should also be integrated. I also thought it would be interesting to include a section about other celebrities who were guest stars on the show early in their careers. Lastly, I wanted to make sure that fans of the show could participate somehow in the publication. To that end, I incorporated a Reader Poll section and Reader Feedback section. I decided that the newsletter would be published on a quarterly basis and would be about ten pages in length. With a tentative design layout completed, I was now ready to move forward with my first issue.

The rest is history with the newsletter being first published in 1995 and continuing until today (2005—In fact, the newsletter has long outlived the original five year network run of the show, lasting over ten years). I thought it would be prudent if I sent the first issue out to all the cast members for them to get an idea of what I was producing. That way, if there was going to be a problem with my publication, I would hear about it pretty quickly. However, the reaction was nothing but positive, and the newsletter has continued with much success and cast endorsements since that time. Although I had some initial fears early on that I would run out of material as time passed, this has not been the case. The show continues to be seen on TV Land by a whole new, third generation of fans and is just as popular now (or more so) than it has ever been.

My purpose in writing this book is to share with all fans the experiences that I have had meeting and getting to know the cast members from *The Dick Van Dyke Show* as I have worked on and published *The Walnut Times*. Some were short encounters—others were more involved. Many of the associations continue today, having evolved into friendships. Subscribers with whom I have shared my experiences in more detail insist that other fans of the show would be very interested in hearing these stories. You can be the judge.

What I can tell you is that it has been a remarkable adventure over the past several years—one which I could have never envisioned when I undertook this endeavor. For a diehard fan of *The Dick Van Dyke Show*, the opportunity to interview and get to personally know the cast has been absolutely awesome and something I will never, ever forget.

I have devoted a separate chapter to each of the main cast members which describes my personal experiences with each of them, in the chronological order that they transpired. These chapters not only include a detailed account of my adventures, but they also feature the comprehensive interviews done at the time. I think you will also find that the other chapters regarding crew members, guest stars, documentaries, and special events provide some additionally interesting insights and unique perspectives.

Hey—I can hear that theme music starting now, can't you? Remember—keep your sense of humor and your thumbs up!

6    TO TWILO AND BEYOND!

Drawing by Michael Wilhelm

# 2

## *Rose Marie*

As I set out to develop the first issue of the newsletter, I decided to contact Rose Marie and ask if she would consider doing a telephone interview with me since she had responded so positively to my initial correspondence. I received a return letter from her within a week's time asking that I send her a tentative list of dates and times for the interview. She indicated that her publicist would get in touch with me to finalize the interview. I picked some dates and possible times and responded immediately.

And then I waited for a reply. Nothing. No letter or contact from anyone. Now what should I do? I decided to wait it out a little bit more. Time passed and I still did not receive any feedback.

About two weeks later, on a Sunday night, the telephone rang, and I heard my wife answer in the other room. "Hold on," she said, "I'll get him for you." I could hear her footsteps coming toward me in the family room. "It's Rose Marie," she said. "I recognize her voice."

I can still remember our first exchange. "Hi, Miss Marie," I said. "It's wonderful to hear from you."

"Please don't call me Miss Marie," she said.

"Okay, Rose," I replied.

"No, no." she responded, "don't call me Rose either. Please just call me Rose Marie."

"You got it!" I blurted back, thinking at this point I would never get it right.

"Do you still want to do an interview with me?" she asked.

"Sure do."

"Let's do it this Wednesday at 3:30 your time," she instructed. "Next time I'm going to call collect!"

"Okay," I replied. "I'm looking forward to talking with you."

As Wednesday approached, I prepared a detailed list of questions that I wanted to ask Rose Marie—not only about *The Dick Van Dyke Show*, but about her career, too. Especially that hair bow that she has ALWAYS worn! Suddenly I felt a little under pressure. I had pushed to get this interview, and now I had a feeling that I might goof it up somehow. Did I have enough questions? Did I have the *right* questions? The last thing I wanted to do was to come off as unprepared or unprofessional!

Wednesday arrived and I sat by phone as the clock ticked closer to 3:30 ET. 3:30 came and went, but no call. 3:45 came and went, but no call. 4:00 came and went—NO CALL! I couldn't imagine what was going on. Had I written down the wrong day? Maybe we got the time zones confused, and Rose Marie would be calling me at 3:30 her time. Another hour passed and there was no call. I didn't even know who to contact to try to straighten things out. My wife tossed out the possibility that maybe she wasn't going to call after all. I waited as patiently as I could for 6:30 ET to arrive hoping that the call would finally come. No call.

For all practical purposes, I gave up for the time being. In a way, I had no choice. I had no direct contact phone number, so I conceded to myself that I would have to send another letter and inquire about what happened.

At 7:30 PM ET, the phone rang. I answered only to hear a voice on the other end of the line ask, "I have a collect call from Rose Marie. Will you accept the charges?"

"I certainly will," I responded, somehow wondering if this call was actually finally happening.

I had hardly answered the operator when I recognized that familiar voice laughing and saying, "I screwed up. Sorry about that. I was visiting my mother at the convalescent home, and I lost all track of time. But, I'm ready to talk now if you are!"

"I sure am. Let's do it!"

I pulled out my list of questions, got situated at my desk, started my tape recorder, and kicked into interview mode. I should probably explain that I had decided early on that it would be smart to record these interviews. Why? Although the quality of the recording wasn't great, the mere fact that I was recording the questions and answers meant that I did not have to be feverishly writing during the interview. That way, I could also be listening astutely and concentrate more on the answers being given—and to formulate an appropriate follow up question. Looking back now, the recordings have become treasured archives for me of these entertainment icons.

TWT: It's well known that you earned the title "Baby Rose Marie" when you were very young. What was your first job in show business?

RM: I won an amateur contest when I was three.

TWT: Was that singing or dancing?

RM: Singing. I've always had the voice that I have now, so it was a little spectacular for a three year old.

TWT: Is that when your trademark of a hair bow began?

RM: The bow is a personal thing and has never been explained.

TWT: Can you tell us what a typical work week was like on *The Dick Van Dyke Show*? Did you all meet on Monday morning with a brand new script?

RM: We met on a Wednesday morning. We would read next week's script, comment on it, Morey would throw in a joke, Sheldon would say, "Dick can't do that, it makes him look too tough…let Morey do that," and Sheldon would criticize it all the way through. Then we would put it aside and start on page one of this week's script. We would go back over each line and each situation and try to get better jokes. After going over the lines, we would get up on our feet and move around. John Rich was our wonderful and brilliant director from the start, and he would tell us "just move around, and, if you're wrong, I'll tell you where you're wrong."

TWT: What transpired the rest of the week?

RM: On Thursday, we would do more formal blocking. On Friday, we would do a "run through" for Carl and Sheldon. Over the weekend we would have a revised script delivered to the house, but nobody looked at it because we knew it was going to change again. On Monday, we would have more revisions. On Tuesday, we would start from the top and go through it with cameras to make sure that everybody had their markings because we worked with three cameras. Then we would break and go get made up, and then we'd go for dinner. The audience would come in at 7:00, we would all be introduced, and we would do the show like a play.

TWT: Did someone warm up the audience prior to the show?

RM: Carl would usually warm up the audience. Then he would introduce Morey and me, and we would do a couple of bits, and then we'd introduce the rest of the cast, and by 7:30 we'd be ready to go to work.

TWT: What would happen if a mistake was made during the filming?

RM: We just backed up two lines and started over from there in front of the audience. And Morey would say "that's why there are dry cleaners and erasers on pencils...we all make mistakes!"

TWT: If you were not in a particular episode, did you still go into work?

RM: No, I got a week off.

TWT: Fans have the impression that the cast got together each week after the show for a cast party. Is this true?

RM: Yes, that's true. After all, we were through at 9:00. So, we'd all go out to some restaurant and have a bite to eat and talk about the show. We also had a lot of birthday parties and anniversary things. Dick and Morey and Mary would all celebrate their birthdays in December and I would have my own birthday party in August!

TWT: Do you have a personal favorite show?

RM: I have quite a few. "Where Have You Been Fassbinder?" which is my birthday party. I love the one when the baby is born. I think that is a classic show. Of course, I pick all the ones I'm in. I like the Vic Damone show and the other show with Guy Marks where I was going to get married and it all turned out to be false.

TWT: Do you think you are most well known for your role as Sally Rogers?

RM: Yes, I'm sure. It's only the older people who remember Baby Rose Marie.

TWT: What kind of impact did the guest stars have on the show?

RM: Generally speaking, if you do a guest shot on a show that's been on a long time, you sort of feel like an outsider because the regular cast has all their things together. But you feel like you're not a part of it because you haven't been there. But we never did that. We made sure that everybody felt as if they'd been on the show for years. We were a very happy group. We had a wonderful group of people.

TWT: It appears to the audience that the musical numbers on the show were performed live. Can you comment on this?

RM: Morey and myself were live and performed with a live pit band which was on the set. Dick and Mary's numbers were taped.

TWT: Do you have any personal memorabilia from the show?

RM: I have a lot of photographs. Every year at Christmas we used to give out gifts to the crew. Dick was a doodler and a wonderful artist, and he made caricatures of all of us. We had that imprinted on an ash tray one year. The following year we had it imprinted on decks of cards, and another year we had it imprinted on cups.

TWT: Do you have any of the more current merchandise which is now available?

RM: I have some of the t-shirts. I asked for them because I get a lot of requests from celebrity auctions.

TWT: Can you tell us about your cast reunion at *Comic Relief* in 1992?

RM: The folks from *Comic Relief* called us up and said that they wanted to honor us. And we were all here, so we went down and did it. The ovation from the crowd was just unbelievable. I think *The Dick Van Dyke Show* is more popular now than it's ever been, because everybody seems to think I'm on the air now. My fan mail has never stopped.

TWT: Do you see much of the other cast members nowadays?

RM: I see Morey quite a bit. We are very, very close. Mary lives in New York, so I don't see her that often. I don't see Dick very often because he lives in Malibu. I was very close to Richard Deacon. He was like a big brother to me. I see John Rich, our director, all the time. I adore that man. I think he is the best comedy director in the business.

As the interview came to a close, I thanked Rose Marie for taking the time to talk with me. A few moments later, the call was over and she was gone.

That was pretty cool, I thought. I just got off the phone with Sally Rogers—Rose Marie from *The Dick Van Dyke Show*! She was absolutely great!

I stopped the tape recorder and quickly rewound it for a short time to check and make sure that I had something to work with. I pressed the "play" button and was *very* happy to hear Rose Marie's voice on the tape.

I spent the next several days listening to and transcribing the questions and answers from the tape. I almost found it more interesting the second time around—I think I was really appreciating the experience much more in retrospect.

I put the finishing touches on the first issue of the newsletter and sent out copies to all the cast members and a handful of subscribers. Of course, I was especially interested in hearing back from Rose Marie—which I did, within a week's time.

"Thank you so much for the Summer 1995 edition of *The Walnut Times* containing our interview," she wrote. "I really enjoyed reading the interview and think it turned out quite well. Continued luck and success in your endeavors."

Little did I know at the time that this short forty-five minute conversation would be the start of a very special friendship which has grown immeasurably since that time.

My first visit to California relative to *The Walnut Times* and gathering material for the newsletter was in January of 1997. My brother-in-law Jack had joined me for the excursion as my "official" photographer. After all, if we were going to meet some cast members, we were certainly going to take lots and lots of photos!

I had sent Rose Marie a note to let her know that we were coming, and she had responded with a letter to tell me that we would try to arrange a meeting of some kind. Unfortunately, no details were ever finalized prior to my departure—and I still did not have a phone number where I could contact her.

What I did have was a phone number for Kay Amsterdam, Morey's wife, who I also hoped to meet during the visit. I called Kay to ask if she would give me Rose Marie's phone number—and she did—so at least I now had a way to get in touch with her.

I dialed Rose Marie's number only to have the line ring several times before an answering machine picked up—and boy was I surprised. The outgoing message had lots and lots of dogs barking and then finally you heard a voice (Rose Marie's voice)—as if it were the dog talking:

"I'm sorry, but our mistress can't come to the phone right now. Leave your number and she'll call you back".

Of course, the significance of this was a demonstration of the care and concern that Rose Marie has for animals in general—but especially Clarence—one of her very, very special canine friends.

I left her a message to let her know that I was in town and was hoping to be able to get together for a short visit and would contact her again. When I did finally reach her the next day, I was disappointed to find out that she was sick with a terrible cold and flat down in bed. The next words out of her mouth was to tell me that Sheldon Leonard had died that day—and this was long before it was announced by the media. I felt a little like an insider. Sheldon and Rose Marie were friends for many years, and his death hit her hard.

Rose Marie explained that she had plans to get to the doctor and might still be able to meet with me, but it didn't look promising.

The trip came to an end without ever being able to get together—but she promised the next time I was "in town" that we'd surely meet up. Fortunately, Rose Marie was well enough to attend Sheldon's funeral a couple of days later and pay tribute to her friend.

Rose Marie's friendship with Sheldon was recognized a few years later when she was asked to unveil a bust of Sheldon at the Disney-MGM Studios in Florida as part of a ceremony related to Sheldon's induction into the Television Academy Hall of Fame. She was very honored to have been asked and extremely happy to participate in the event.

The next opportunity to actually meet Rose Marie came in February 1999. This time, my friend Fred joined me on this trip after much cajoling, with me telling him he would more than likely have the chance to join me in meeting many of these television icons.

I called Rose Marie after our arrival and asked about getting together.

"I'd like to meet you for lunch, but I can't go out in public. I have a terrible sty in my eye," she said. "I look absolutely awful. Unless…maybe I could wear big dark sunglasses."

"I don't care what you wear as long as we can finally meet you," I responded, not wanting to even think that another trip to California would prove unsuccessful in my attempt to finally meet Sally Rogers!

"Alright, I guess we can get together. But we can't take any pictures with my eye looking like this. Let's meet tomorrow for lunch at Jerry's Deli," she said.

"Sounds terrific," I replied. "We'll see you tomorrow at 2."

We arrived at Jerry's Deli no later than 1:45 and went inside to see if Rose Marie had already arrived. Nope. She wasn't there. As the minutes ticked closer to two o'clock, we went back outside to enjoy the warm, California sunshine on this beautiful February day.

Before we realized it, it was now after two o'clock and Rose Marie had still not arrived. Did we miss her arrival somehow? Was there another entrance that she could have used? Maybe she already was inside, and we had just not seen her. It was déjà vu all over again—just like the original telephone interview.

Fred kept watch for her to arrive from out on the sidewalk while I went back inside to see if she had already sat down in the restaurant. As I walked past the deli counter toward the hostess stand, I heard an announcement over the loud speaker.

"Phone call for David Van Deusen. Please come to the hostess desk."

I took a few more steps and was at the stand asking for the phone.

"Hello…"

"David, this is Rose Marie. You're at the other Jerry's Deli."

"What? The other Jerry's Deli? What are you talking about?"

She continued. "There are two of them on Sepulveda—one on the lower part where you are, and one on the upper part where I am. I didn't think of it until just now when I realized we hadn't pinned down the exact one."

"We'll be right there," I said. "Will you wait for us?"

"Sure. I'll be here." She let out a laugh. "You'll recognize me with my big sunglasses on."

Fred and I hopped in the car and sped up Ventura to the other Jerry's. I use the word "sped" loosely—as it seemed to take forever in the lanes of "backed up" traffic that we encountered. We finally reached "the other" Jerry's—which was right next door to a Kinko's Copy Center. You'll see the relevance of Kinko's soon.

When we walked through the front door, there was Rose Marie with giant sunglasses and all, waiting for us, with a manila folder in hand. The hostess started to lead us to our table when Rose Marie gave her instructions to take us to the back of the restaurant to a big table where we could have a little privacy and talk.

As we sat down in the large booth, Rose Marie leaned over quietly and gave me a nudge.

"Take a look at this, will ya." She lowered her sunglasses just enough to give me a peek at the eye. And she was right. She had a major sty in her eye. It looked awful.

"See what I mean? There was no way I was coming out looking like this—without wearing sunglasses, that is!"

We placed our lunch orders and began to chat. Fred and I were all ears as Rose Marie began to tell us stories about her career.

She described what it was like to be a performer in the original nightclubs of Las Vegas—and have Bugsy Siegel as her boss. Her recollections were vivid and very interesting.

The stories continued on a variety of subjects as lunch came. Rose Marie pulled out the manila folder and reached inside to pull out several vintage photos of her and her friends. First, there was one of her at age sixteen. Then came the others—Morey Amsterdam, Ethel Merman, Frank Sinatra, Richard Deacon, Phil Silvers, and Rocky Graziano, just to name a few. I thought to myself—maybe she'll let me borrow them so I could use them in the newsletter. As quickly as I thought it, I dismissed the idea.

These were her original photos, and there was no way she was going to loan them to me. She would be concerned that she would never get them back.

As our one and a half hour lunch finished up, we left the restaurant to head toward our respective cars. I looked up to see the Kinko's sign staring me right in the face. There it is! The opportunity to get some copies of her photos. Take a shot and go for it!

"Rose Marie," I muttered. "Would it be okay if I took your photos over to that Kinko's on the way out and had some quick copies made of them? Fred will wait here with you while I do it." I glanced quickly at Fred to see if he was catching on.

"As long as it doesn't take too long," she said. She looked over at Fred. "I knew he was going to like these pictures!"

I dashed into the store and had the copies made as quickly as I could. When I returned, I found that Rose Marie had already gotten in her car and was just waiting for the folder so she could get on her way. We had an enjoyable lunch with intriguing conversation, and I even had some great collectibles now in the form of these color photocopies. But I still didn't have a keepsake photo of Rose Marie and me together.

As I handed her the folder, I smiled a little and took a chance.

"How about a quick photo of you and me? You can keep your glasses on if you want. But I didn't come all the way to California to meet you and have lunch with you and NOT get my picture taken with you!"

She turned her head and gave a smile. "You are really something! Come on, let's take a picture."

I angled myself in next to the driver's window of her bright red car and Fred snapped the photo.

"Thanks for a very nice lunch," she said. "I really enjoyed it."

"We did, too! Now you take care of yourself." I leaned my head through the window and gave her a kiss on the cheek—and then away she drove.

Fred and I had a wonderful time—and Rose Marie was an absolute pisser with all of her jokes and stories.

Upon my return home, I began to put together an issue on Rose Marie's career. From her beginnings as Baby Rose Marie through her touring with *4 Girls 4*, it was an extremely interesting look at the history of show business through one person's seventy year career. To top it off, the copies of the photos that I had been fortunate to get at our lunch were perfect to accompany the article.

Rose Marie and I continued to stay in touch through occasional phone calls, but mostly through letters we exchanged every few months—generally around the release of a new issue of the newsletter. I saw her again in the summer of 2000 when she participated in my "The Making of 'It May Look Like a Walnut'" video. That meeting is detailed in a separate chapter about the video (see Chapter 13).

I sent congratulations to Rose Marie on October 3, 2001, the day she received her star on the Hollywood Walk of Fame. Interestingly, this date was also the 40th Anniversary of the premier of *The Dick Van Dyke Show*. Was it a coincidence?? Who knows? In any case, it was a very special day for Rose Marie. Carl was there to recognize her accomplishment as was

Dick and his vocal quartet. They sang an "a cappella" arrangement of *The Dick Van Dyke Show* theme to honor her—more on that later.

In September, 2002, I made another trip to Los Angeles with a plan to meet with several of the cast. When I arrived in town, I called Rose Marie to see if she had any free time in her schedule. At the time of my call, she was waiting for her daughter Georgiana to come by to help review the galley proofs of her soon-to-be-published autobiography, *Hold the Roses,* and she expressed to me that she wasn't sure if she would have time for a lunch date during my visit. I told her that I had a 1960s magazine article to drop off to her about her and her husband, Bobby Guy, which was published shortly after Bobby's untimely death. I told her I was only minutes from her home and asked if I could just drop it by the house. She agreed.

When I stopped by the house, she opened the door and motioned me inside. "Come on in," she said.

"I don't want to interrupt progress on your book," I replied, and remained with feet firmly planted on the front stoop.

"Come on in," she repeated, in a somewhat more authoritative tone.

"Okay," I said, as she led me through the living room to the kitchen where we sat down at the table, and proceeded to have an hour long conversation.

We talked about her autobiography, and she showed me the finalized cover design. Her book was ultimately published later that year by Kentucky University Press, and if you haven't read it, you should pick up a copy. The writing is such that it is as if you are sitting with Rose Marie listening to her tell you all about of her adventures in show business—from age three to the present.

She went on to tell me how Carl had recently called and asked her to work on the upcoming *Alan Brady Animated Show* with him and Dick. She told me of her brother's recent death and shared other remembrances of her friendship with Richard Deacon. She also asked about what I was up to and about my family. We had a nice time getting caught up on what was happening in each other's lives.

As we wrapped up our chat and I headed down the front path to my car in the driveway, I came to the realization that our affiliation had evolved into more than just that of "newsletter publisher" and "celebrity." Somehow, over the years through the creation of this fan publication, Rose Marie and I had become *very* good friends. Not only had we shared *Dick Van Dyke Show* interests and related memories, but we had also exchanged personal sentiments during the loss of my parents, Morey's death, and the passing of her dear mother. We had gotten to know each other's families and were genuinely interested in each other's well being. It had become a very special relationship.

I have since experienced many other marvelous adventures with Rose Marie, including the TV Land Awards in 2003 and *The Dick Van Dyke Show Revisited* in 2004. Each of these events is covered in detail later in this book in their own respective chapters.

I am very proud to call Rose Marie my "friend" and I know that she feels the same way. The unique bond that we share is one that I deeply cherish and will treasure forever.

# 3

## *Morey Amsterdam*

My first personal contact with Morey Amsterdam came to fruition thanks to Rose Marie.

I had tried to locate Morey through the Screen Actor's Guild, but he no longer had an agent at eighty-six years of age. Imagine that!

Since I knew that Rosie and Morey were still the best of friends, I asked Rose Marie what would be the best way to get in touch with him.

"Here's his number," she said. "Give him a call. I'm sure he'll be happy to talk with you."

Now I'm not a guy who is easily intimidated, but I'm honest enough to tell you that I felt a little funny about just calling Morey up right out of the blue. All I could imagine was Morey thinking—who is this guy? What does he want from me?

I finally decided that I should just give him a call and see what would happen. The worst he could do was hang up on me. Right?

So one day in 1995, I picked up the phone and dialed his number. As the phone rang in the ear piece, I collected my thoughts and got my little spiel ready. One ring…two rings…three rings…no answer yet.

Click—the line picked up—but it was Morey's answering machine. As I poised myself to leave my information, the outgoing message was interrupted by a live voice.

"Hello." It was Morey.

"May I speak to Mr. Amsterdam?"

"This is he."

"Mr. Amsterdam, my name is David Van Deusen," I blurted out. "Rose Marie gave me your number." I figured if I let him know that Rose Marie was the one who gave me his phone number that he'd be more inclined to at least hear me out and not hang up on me. What I discovered moments later was that I had nothing at all to worry about.

"Yes," said Morey. "What can I do for you?"

I proceeded to tell Morey about my publication and how I had done an interview with Rose Marie for my very first issue—and that I'd like to do an interview with him for my second installment.

"Would that be in person or by phone?" he asked.

"It would be by phone as I'm out in Albany, New York."

"Oh yes," Morey chuckled, "Right near Amsterdam, New York!"

"That's right!" I said.

And so we were off and running. Even in the first few moments of a phone call to someone I had never met, Morey's comic timing and sense of humor came shining through.

A couple of weeks later when I called Morey again to talk with him, his wife Kay was preparing Chicken Kiev for dinner. The initial part of our conversation was relative to what a wonderful fifty-four year marriage he and Kay had experienced. His remarks were genuine and sweet, all at the same time. We then moved on to begin to talk about his widely varied, multi-decade career—including his five years on *The Dick Van Dyke Show*.

TWT: How did you come to be known as the "Human Joke Machine?"

MA: I used to do a bit in one of my shows where I would wear what looked like a hand organ. I would go through the audience as a "joke box." And anything that the audience called out I would pretend to write down, put it in the joke box, and turn the handle. Then out came a piece of paper, and I would read the joke produced by the joke box. Of course, there was nothing on the paper because I made it up on the spot. Believe it or not, I started getting letters from people wanting to know where they could buy "one of those joke boxes." I guess they thought it would be a big hit at parties.

TWT: How did you land the role of Buddy Sorrel?

MA: I had been writing for years for Rose Marie, and she had already been selected to play Sally Rogers. She suggested to Carl Reiner that I be considered for the role. Carl called and asked if I could come out from

New York the next day to do a pilot. Since I was in the middle of shoveling my car out of the snow, I told him I would leave in five minutes. I had to do something to get away from the god damn snow.

TWT: What were you doing in New York at that time?

MA: Doing television and personal appearances. I had a nightclub in New York for five years, and I also had a restaurant across the street from Carnegie Hall.

TWT: Was this the job that moved you to California permanently?

MA: Yes, it was. My wife and I first rented an apartment and, shortly thereafter, bought a home. In fact, my wife and I are still living in the same house that I bought in 1961.

TWT: Can you tell us once and for all, what is your real birthday?

MA: I was born December 14, 1908. But you know, every year when they announce my birthday on TV, they give me a different age.

TWT: What other interesting things can you tell us about yourself?

MA: I hold the world's record for having done seventy-five shows in one week. I was on radio and television at the time with NBC. Between my radio, TV, and live appearances, I managed to accumulate seventy-five shows in one week. I played Madison Square Garden so often I used to say it was my room.

TWT: Please tell us about your family.

MA: My wife, Kay, and I go everywhere together. She is a very successful interior decorator, having decorated all of the executive offices at Radio City. We have two children. My son is in the picture business and also in the photography business. My daughter is a psychologist and is married to a psychiatrist.

TWT: Can you tell us something about your musical background?

MA: I came from a musical family. My father was the concertmaster for the San Francisco Symphony for thirty-five years. And as a result my mother became an international cook. My father would call and say he was bringing Pablo Casals home for dinner, and she would make Spanish food. Or he would bring Caruso home, and she would make Italian food. Consequently, we had all of the famous opera stars and concert artists as guests in our home.

TWT: How would you describe your experiences on *The Dick Van Dyke Show?*

MA: Being on *The Dick Van Dyke Show* was a lucky break for me being with such talented people. I never saw any temperament. Nobody ever argued with anybody, and there was never a cross word. We were one big happy family and remain close friends to this day.

TWT: Do you have a favorite episode?

MA: Mine is the "Bar Mitzvah" show. Let me tell you how that came to be. One day at lunch several of us were talking about what funny things happened at our Bar Mitzvah. And Carl asked me about mine. I told him that I was never Bar Mitzvahed. As a result, Carl sat down and wrote the show for me, and it turned out to be a tremendous success.

TWT: The ceremony seemed very realistic.

MA: Let me tell you about that. Carl decided we were going to have a real cantor for the Bar Mitzvah. So he looked one up in the synagogue near the studio and hired him for the part. When the cantor started to sing the prayers and he looked up to see an audience of four hundred people, suddenly the "ham" in him came out (of course, that's funny to say about a cantor), and he went on and on for about ten minutes. When he paused for a second, I yelled "one more time!"

TWT: Tell us about some of your musical credits.

MA: I wrote "Rum and Coca-Cola" for the Andrews Sisters. And I wrote "Why Did I Ever Leave Wyoming?" as a cowboy song, and it is now the state song of Wyoming.

TWT: I understand you've written comedy material for some of the best.

MA: You're probably talking to the only guy who ever wrote for Will Rogers. Will Rogers came in to play a theatre where I was performing. In those days, we all had rotten dressing rooms. There was a mirror, a shelf, a chair, an army cot, and a sink. There was only one toilet on every floor. Well, the toilet on our floor was the noisiest toilet you ever heard. When you flushed it, it sounded like the whole building was falling down. So I went down to the stage manager and asked him to make me a sign, and I hung it up by the toilet. The sign said "If you are constipated, flush the toilet first…it will scare the shit out of you!" Well, Will Rogers came in and saw the sign, and he got hysterical. He went down and asked the stage manager who put the sign in there. From then on, we were buddies. He was such a delightful guy. I gave many, many gags to Will, and he always gave me credit. I worked with him until the day he was killed.

TWT: Do you have any personal memorabilia from the *Van Dyke Show*?

MA: Yes, I have the hats that I wore in the show, as well as a collection of about thirty vests. I also have some scripts from the show. I think one of my hats and vests are in the Smithsonian.

TWT: How close in character was Buddy Sorrel to Morey Amsterdam?

MA: I was playing myself. I've been a comedy writer all my life. I'm also a concert cellist. And I think anybody who manages to be able to do the things they like has got it made.

TWT: One of the classic *Dick Van Dyke Show* episodes enjoyed by fans is "The Ghost of A. Chantz" where Buddy was really spooked!

MA: Do you know I nearly got killed in that episode? Do you remember when I got on the bed and it curled up? Some guy pressed the wrong button, and it started to close up on me when I wasn't ready for it.

TWT: What comments can you pass on to us about the other cast members?

MA: We had great people to work with. Carl Reiner is an absolute genius. And Dick Van Dyke is one of the most talented guys I know. Did you know that he plays classical piano? Between shots he used to go over and sit down and play Bach fugues. Dick is a very warm, nice guy. Of course, I don't see Mary often because she lives in New York. I think she is one of the best straight women I have ever seen. As a matter of fact, in all of the years that we were together, she only told me one joke. Rose Marie and I continue to be very close friends after all these years.

TWT: I've heard about your video room. Can you tell me about it?

MA: The room holds my awards and collection of photos. It also holds my collection of vintage movies and early radio programs. I have four VCRs including the ¾" format as well as the ½" inch format. I pretty much have a complete video room. I could shoot a film in there! Right now, I'm working on something for Steve Allen which chronicles old vaudeville acts. Many people remember the acts but don't remember anything specific about them. I'm fortunate to have many of them on film.

TWT: Obviously, you're not considering retiring.

MA: I work when I feel like it. In the wintertime, I don't go east because I don't like the snow, but, outside of that, I'm as busy as I want to be. I'm working on my autobiography now. It's called *I Remember Me*. The other day somebody said to me "How would you like to live your life over again?" and I said I couldn't afford it with the price of everything today!

TWT: What would you like your fans to remember about you?

MA: I lead a very happy life, and I'm fortunate to have a great family and good friends in all lines of business. I like everybody, and I learn a little bit from everybody. So that's my life, that's what I do, and I enjoy doing what I do.

As the interview concluded, Morey thanked *me* for wanting to interview *him*, and told me if I had any more questions to feel free to give him a call—anytime. In a brief one hour phone call, I really felt as if we had become friends.

Morey subsequently took the time to send me an autographed copy of his *Cookbook for Drinkers* as well as a copy of the lyrics that he wrote to *The Dick Van Dyke Show* theme song. Little did anyone know, including Earle Hagen himself, that Morey had written words to go along with Hagen's catchy melody and called the composition "Keep Your Fingers Crossed." (Remember that song that Dick and his quartet sang at Rose Marie's Walk of Fame ceremony? As I said earlier, more on this song later in the book.)

In the months that followed our initial conversation and the publishing of Morey's interview in the fall of 1995, Morey would often phone me out of the blue just to say hello and to tell me a joke. On one occasion, he was very amused to discover that a joke he had written about two weeks before had gone full circle around Los Angeles and had come back to him through the telling of his joke to him by another comedian. It was shortly after the October 1995 decision in the famous O.J. Simpson trial when Morey called with the following:

Photo courtesy of Kay Amsterdam

"Authorities have discovered that Adolph Hitler is not dead but has been in hiding for years. In fact, he has been arrested and will be tried for all of the atrocities and war crimes which he committed." Morey's narration continued. "The only problem is that they are going to try the case in Los Angeles County!"

He laughed and I laughed. This joke was just one more of the thousands that Morey had in the Rolodex in his brain. He was simply amazing. Morey's enthusiasm continued to bubble over as he went on to tell me about a deal he had cut with Nick-at-Nite to produce short thirty second spots for the network which would be called "Thoughts While Not Thinking." Morey always had a special way of looking at things, didn't he?

One of the more unique merchandise items I produced for *The Walnut Times* was the Morey Amsterdam baseball cap. Morey gave permission for me to imprint his caricature on a cap and make it available to subscribers of the newsletter and fans of the show. All he asked for in return was for me to send him a few of the hats so he would be able to sign and donate them to celebrity fund raising events. He even agreed to have his picture taken wearing the hat! Pretty cool. So I quickly obliged after my order of hats was produced and sent Morey some for his use.

In August 1996, I picked up my mail to find a great photo of Morey sporting the "Morey Amsterdam hat." It was just fabulous! Morey had also returned two of the caps to me with his autograph—one for me to keep for my private collection and one to be used as a subscriber prize.

I called to thank Morey for the photo and went on to explain that I was planning to make a trip to California in January of the coming year. I asked if he might consider meeting with me during my stay.

"Sure," he spouted, "let's get together for a cup of coffee. I'll buy!"

Sadly, just two months before my visit, Morey was stricken by a fatal heart attack. He was nearly eighty-eight years young at the time of his death in October 1996.

In the time that has elapsed since Morey has passed, I have established and maintained a wonderful friendship with Kay Amsterdam, Morey's wife of fifty-four years. I continue to send Kay the newsletter, we talk every few months on the telephone, and we also exchange holiday greeting cards.

Kay tells the story of one of Morey's favorite Christmas cards which depicts a distant shot of the manger in Bethlehem with everyone gathered round waiting to hear the news of the birth, just as someone shouts "It's a girl!"

*The Walnut Times* Morey Amsterdam hat, signed for me by Morey

Speaking of Christmas cards, Morey worked out a deal for many years with the Postmaster in Amsterdam, New York, to get the "Amsterdam" postmark on each of his cards. Morey would send one giant package which contained all of the cards, fully addressed with postage affixed, to the Amsterdam post office. Upon receipt at the office, the package would be opened and each card postmarked "Amsterdam" for that special, extra added touch.

Kay called me shortly after the first annual TV Land Awards aired in March 2003, and remarked that she had watched the show with great interest as *The Dick Van Dyke Show* cast was honored with the TV Legend Award. Rose Marie had acknowledged Morey during her acceptance remarks, and Kay appreciated Rosie's comments and thoughts about Morey and all that he brought to the show. Kay's only disappointment was that Morey was not here to be recognized and receive this award along with his co-stars.

As I reflected on Kay's thoughts, I wondered what I might be able to do to help remedy this situation. I have often felt that Rose Marie's and Morey's contributions to the success of *The Dick Van Dyke Show* are not acknowledged or are overlooked by critics who write about the show's endurance and quality.

I got in touch with Sal Maniaci at TV Land and conveyed the feelings expressed by Kay. I asked if he might consider sending Kay a letter to acknowledge Morey's key participation in the show. Leave it to Sal, he did one better! Sal had another TV Land Legend Award engraved with Morey's name and sent it on to Kay as a posthumous acknowledgement of Morey's integral role on *The Dick Van Dyke Show*. What a wonderful tribute!

I continue to keep in touch with Kay to this day, and our discussions often focus on the impact that Morey had in show business during his nearly nine decades of entertaining.

I did not know Morey for very long, yet he still left a lasting impression on me. I remember him fondly for his "always positive outlook" and his love of life—and, of course, his famous quote "I'm the happiest fella I've ever met." I'm sure he left us with a joke on the tip of his tongue and a smile on his face.

# 4

## *Ann Guilbert*

I was continuing in my quest to contact as many cast members as I could who were associated with the show to attempt to set up telephone interviews. Two issues had been completed at this point, and I needed to line up another cast member for the main interview in the next edition.

I had sent a letter to Ann Guilbert (who by the way, dropped the "Morgan" part of her name many years before), and Ann had responded to me and indicated that I should call her agent to set up a time for us to chat. As such, I called Bauman/Hiller and Associates in Los Angeles and asked to speak with Ann's agent.

Ann's agent came on the line, and I explained that I had written to Ann and was interested in doing an interview with her about her role as Millie on *The Dick Van Dyke Show*. The agent said she would give Ann a call and get back to me.

I was stunned when the phone rang back a few minutes later to have the agent say that Ann was available "right now" to talk with me. Not knowing if or when I might get another opportunity to speak with Ann, I told the agent that we could do the interview right away. That said, I knew I was only semi-prepared since I had not yet developed a full list of questions to ask Ann.

A few minutes later, the phone rang, and it was Ann calling me back. I began, somewhat by the seat of my pants, to conduct the interview.

TWT: How did you land the role of Millie Helper?

AG: Jerry Paris was a friend of my former husband, so I knew Jerry for a long time before *The Dick Van Dyke Show*. Jerry had gotten the role of the neighbor, and they needed a wife for him. So he mentioned me and took me down to audition for Carl Reiner and Sheldon Leonard.

TWT: Were you the only actress who auditioned for the role?

AG: You know, I don't have any idea. Jerry had told me at one point that Carl Reiner didn't think I was pretty enough. But Carl had seen me do a musical review and knew my work. In any case, he hired me. But I'm sure Jerry helped me to get the job. In other words, I knew somebody.

TWT: We continue to hear about the integral roles that Carl Reiner and Sheldon Leonard played in making the show a success. Can you give us your impression of the impact that they had on the show?

AG: I didn't know Sheldon nearly as well as I knew Carl. Carl really was the "daddy" of the show. Everything was basically his idea and his personality and everything that kept it such a great working place. Sheldon, of course, was the Executive Producer and had several shows on at the time. Sheldon had a sixth sense about stories, so he would come down and say what was wrong with the story and how it needed to work better.

TWT: Can you tell us about the relationships that you had with the other cast members?

AG: Because I worked the most with Mary, I think I probably spent the most time with her when we weren't involved in a scene. And of course, when he wasn't acting, I would spend time with Jerry.

TWT: What did you do during your free time on the set?

AG: We used to play Perquackey. Basically I remember doing it with John Rich and Mary. John and Mary and I were fanatics. I remember one time I kept winning over Mary. She cornered me in the prop room, and we must have played Perquackey for three or four hours before she finally won. All the while she was saying, "Don't let me win, don't let me win!"

TWT: Do you still keep in touch with Mary today?

AG: No, I haven't seen her or talked to her for many, many years.

TWT: Do you watch the show in reruns?

AG: I watch it very rarely. I think the fans of the show know more about it than I do. It's been a long time, you know. I have some of the shows on tape, but not nearly anywhere near all of them.

TWT: Do you have a favorite *Dick Van Dyke Show* episode?

AG: My favorite is the one I had the biggest part in! It was one where Rob and Jerry went fishing ("Long Night's Journey into Day") when there was a burglar in the neighborhood, and we heard this noise and we were terrified. Of course, it was Rob coming home, but we didn't know that! That was the one I had the most fun doing. Jerry Paris's favorite show was "It May Look Like a Walnut."

TWT: We understand that you were expecting during the course of the show. How was that handled?

AG: It wasn't even mentioned. I was expecting my daughter, Hallie Todd, who is now an actress. I talked to Carl and told him that I was pregnant. He was great and very easy going…and he decided to just wing it. So I worked until I was about seven months pregnant. And since the baby wasn't very big, it was hardly noticeable.

TWT: Do you have personal mementos that you saved from the show?

AG: I don't really have too much, but I do have some photos and newspaper clippings. I have one thing that I'm saving and treasuring, and that is a double deck of cards. Dick had made a caricature of the cast and had it printed on a deck of cards. I still have the unopened, pristine deck of cards.

TWT: Fans continue to enjoy your role of Grandma Yetta on *The Nanny*. How did you land this role?

AG: I went and auditioned for it. In other words, I didn't know anybody. There was no Jerry Paris to help me out on this one!

TWT: How does this part compare to others that you have played?

AG: I have a lot of fun. I have more fun than I have had in my life.

TWT: Is Grandma Yetta the most fun you have had playing a role?

AG: It is the most fun I have had playing a role on television, but I have done a lot of theater.

TWT: What was your favorite theater role?

AG: I think maybe *'night, Mother*. I did *'night, Mother* at Arena Stage in Washington, DC. I get my main jollies from the theater.

TWT: With all the roles that you have played over the course of your career, do you think you are best known as Millie Helper?

AG: Oh yeah, no doubt. I can't get rid of that broad. But I think it has certainly helped me as I look back thirty-five years later. Many television writers are big fans of the show, another whole generation. For most of the writers, *The Dick Van Dyke Show* is one of their very favorite shows. If you had something to do with the show, they tend to listen to you a little more.

TWT: How would you summarize your overall perception of the show?

AG: I think *The Dick Van Dyke Show* has held up pretty well. The laughs weren't dated. They didn't use contemporary things and they kept it in a life situation.

I have already made it clear that this interview was arranged for very quickly, without hardly any notice at all. What that also meant was that all three of my children, ages eight, six, and two and a half at the time, were also at home and otherwise engaged in doing things of their own, while I was attempting to conduct the interview.

Right smack during the interview, my youngest daughter came to me and interrupted the phone conversation. I excused myself briefly to talk with my daughter, all the while wondering how Ann would react to the interruption.

Her immediate response was to ask, "Is that your daughter I hear talking? How old is she? She sounds close to the age of my granddaughter?"

It became quickly obvious that, although Ann was a celebrity, she was also a very nice, down-to-earth lady and genuinely interested in also learning about me and my family.

I thanked Ann for her time as we finished up the interview and told her I would be in touch.

During my first to trip to Los Angeles, Ann invited Jack and me to attend a taping of *The Nanny*. She gave me directions to the studio and told me she would meet us outside after the taping was completed.

The episode was very funny, and Ann had some great lines during the show. After the episode was finished, she motioned to me in the bleachers to tell me she would be right out to see us. But before I continue, I need to fill you in concerning the "giant walnut."

Shortly after I started the newsletter, I stumbled upon a giant sized candy dish which was in the shape and brownish color of a walnut. The item was ceramic and subtly larger than a plump grapefruit, with separate top and bottom pieces which fit loosely together, one half on top of the other. Let's put it this way—any overgrown chipmunk would have killed to have had this nut in his storage for the winter!

I had decided to bring the "giant walnut" candy dish along with me on my trip, thinking it would be a great prop to hold in the photos that I would have taken of me with the cast members from the show. Okay—on with the story!

As promised, Ann arrived outside a few minutes later to visit with us, having ditched her Yetta costume and wig in favor of street clothes and a bandana on her head. We talked for a good half hour, and, as the conversation came to a close, I asked if we could take a couple of photos.

"Would you mind holding the giant walnut in the photo?" I asked?

"The giant walnut?" she replied. "What's that?"

I reached into my bag and carefully pulled out the ceramic candy dish.

"This is the giant walnut," I said. "I thought it would be fun to include it in our photo as a remembrance of the walnut episode."

She laughed. "Yes, the episode that I didn't have a part in! But that's okay!"

I handed Ann the walnut dish and turned toward Jack to see if he was just about ready to take the photos. Just then, I heard it. A loud, hollow sounding "pop."

I spun around to see the top half of the dish, in several pieces, lying at my feet, on the cement sidewalk.

"Oh no," exclaimed Ann. "The top piece slipped off the bottom, right out of my hand. I hope you have another one of these."

"No," I responded. "As far as I know, it's one of a kind."

I leaned down to assess the damage. Fortunately, the walnut had broken into three large pieces with several smaller chips missing from some of the edges. I picked up the pieces and held them together as best as I could for our photo.

Ann, Jack, and I all had a quite a laugh about the "cracking" of the giant walnut. The most ironic part about this whole thing? The photo that we took was underexposed and didn't even come out! I should tell you that upon returning home, I was able to glue the pieces of the dish back together. And despite a few missing chips, it has continued as a unique symbol of the newsletter to this day!

As the years have passed, Ann and I have also become pretty good friends. On my subsequent visits to Los Angeles she invited me back to the set of *The Nanny* to see the taping of another episode. She also told me about a favorite diner of hers called Patrick's Roadhouse, as she thought I'd enjoy having breakfast there during my stay in LA. Patrick's is easily recognizable for its bright green shamrock-like color and is located on the Pacific Coast Highway between Santa Monica and the Palisades. Although it's not very fancy, it is a well known celebrity hang out. Arnold Schwarzenegger has his own personal table at the restaurant!

The first opportunity I had to stop by Patrick's was in the summer of 2000 when I was in town with my family to shoot the "Making of 'It May Look Like a Walnut'" video.

We stopped there for breakfast one morning, and, as we sat down, I told the woman that the diner had been recommended to us by Ann Guilbert. The lady responded with a puzzled look as if she didn't know who I was talking about.

"You know, Mrs. Fanelli," I said, making reference to a television role that Ann had played many years later—and the role that Ann said the folks from the diner recognized her for playing.

"Oh yes," she replied, "I know who you mean now. Ann was just in a few days ago for breakfast. She enjoys sitting outside on the deck and doing her crossword puzzles while she's here."

"The next time she comes in," I suggested, "please tell her that the walnut guy took her advice and stopped by for breakfast."

A couple of weeks after we returned from our trip, I received a letter from Ann which told the following story.

"Not long after you went to Patrick's, I went for my usual breakfast. Tracey, the owner, told me someone had come in—a guy with his family, who said I had recommended Patrick's to him. She said this guy told her I'd know who he was if she mentioned chipmunk or something. After five minutes of quizzing, I said WALNUTS??? And she said YES! So from now on, it's *The Chipmunk Times* to me!"

In September, 2002, Ann and I finally met each other for breakfast at Patrick's Roadhouse. We sat out on the deck and enjoyed the view of the ocean, the bright California sunshine, the balmy breeze, and, best of all, some delightful conversation about our families and *Dick Van Dyke Show* friends.

Ann is a wonderful lady and has also become a good friend. She is often in New York doing theatre work, and we both keep saying that we'll get together for lunch during one of her stays in the city. But if we don't link up in NYC, you can be sure we'll try to get together again at Patrick's on my next visit to Los Angeles.

# 5

## *Sheldon Leonard*

I can still recall the day that Sheldon Leonard called the house to schedule an interview with me about his involvement with *The Dick Van Dyke Show*. My son, who was six at the time, almost never answered the telephone, but for some reason, on this day, he decided he should answer.

My wife and I were in the other room and quickly glanced at each other when the phone stopped after only one ring. Hearing our son carry on a one-sided conversation around the corner, my wife suggested that I better pick up the phone and see who was calling.

"Hello," I said.

"David?" That one word with that distinctive timbre was all I needed to hear to know who was on the other end of the line. He continued, "This is Sheldon Leonard."

After all, is there any other voice as recognizable as Sheldon Leonard's? It was unmistakable…to me, of course. My six year old had no idea he was conversing with Big Max Calvada—one of the biggest icons the television medium has ever known.

Leonard continued, "Call me Saturday morning and we'll talk. Here's my number…"

I wrote down the number, and, a few seconds later, he was gone. And little did I know at the time, but that was "classic" Sheldon. Here one second and gone the next. He had an amazing ability to slip in and out without being noticed. He was often accused of doing a vanishing act…whether on the set of his TV shows or at the meeting of the Director's Guild of America.

The following Saturday I got set up and made the call to Beverly Hills. A female voice answered the phone.

"Leonard residence," she said.

"Good morning," I said. "My name is David Van Deusen, and I have a 9:00 appointment to do a telephone interview with Mr. Leonard."

"I'm sorry," she replied, "He is not here right now but should be here shortly. Why don't you try him again in a few minutes?" she suggested.

"Would you please let him know that I called?" I wanted to make sure that Sheldon was aware that I had called at the agreed upon time. She took my name and the call ended.

A half hour passed, and I dialed his number again. This time a male voice answered the phone—and again, there was no doubt who it was.

"Hi Mr. Leonard. It's David Van Deusen from *The Walnut Times* calling to do our phone interview." Sheldon was all apologies.

"I'm sorry I was not here earlier when you called," Sheldon explained. "I had gone out with the confident expectation that I would be back in time for your call, but I didn't count on getting a ticket from a traffic cop!"

Amazing. An eighty-nine year old man speeding in and around Beverly Hills. We both had a laugh, and then I got going on the list of questions that I had prepared. Sheldon was just as gracious as I had heard that he would be. Although he had said he would allocate thirty minutes for the phone interview, the conversation easily lasted fifty minutes or more with him providing detailed remembrances of his time with Carl, Dick, Mary, Rosie, Morey, and the rest of the cast and crew.

TWT: Describe your role in the production of *The Dick Van Dyke Show*.

SL: As you probably know, Carl Reiner had originally cast himself in the role of Rob Petrie. But I felt Carl wasn't the right actor to play the part. Carl was a "larger than life" figure, and he didn't conveniently fit into American living rooms and bedrooms. His style was that of a sketch actor where a degree of exaggeration was required. That was incompatible with the television medium. After some discussion, Carl and I agreed that Dick Van Dyke was closer to the concept of what we had in mind.

TWT: How did you fit into the day to day activities of the show?

SL: I directed the pilot and earliest episodes. My responsibility to the show, aside from getting it on the air, was to find the proper director and assist in the selection of a writing staff. In order to do that, I called on my experience with my previous comedy shows, *The Andy Griffith Show* and *The Danny Thomas Show*. One of the key people I selected was director John Rich.

TWT: We understand you formed your own production company to make the show.

SL: Carl, Danny, Dick and I created CALVADA Productions (CA for Carl, VA for Van Dyke, L for Leonard, and DA for Danny).

TWT: From time to time we see the word CALVADA appear in several different episodes.

SL: That was Carl's idea of an inside joke. There was a billboard in one episode that stated "Drink CALVADA". And then there was the role I played called Big Max Calvada.

TWT: Tell us about it.

SL: There was a concept of a show in which a hoodlum intimidates the staff of the show. Once the character role had been decided on, everyone felt I should play the part. Besides, I work cheaper than most actors. Carl, with his perverted sense of humor, kept retreating to calling everything that could bear the label Calvada, hence the mob figure's name became "Big Max Calvada."

TWT: Do you have a favorite personal episode?

SL: Yes, I do. The episode I am about to describe had a very important effect on the future of television. I'm speaking of the episode where Greg Morris shows up with the baby that Dick Van Dyke thinks should be his ("That's My Boy!"). That was a very important episode in many respects. First, it was a very well received episode, but it also had a critical role in allowing me to get Bill Cosby on the air as the first black man in a leading role in a television series. The reaction to Greg Morris was so favorable that it helped me to overcome the network's reluctance to use blacks in prominent roles. Up until that time in the early 1960's, there was still quite a bit of segregation in the south. Blacks were cast as servants or cooks, but they were not put on a level with whites. Happily, the acceptance of Greg Morris on the *Van Dyke Show* and the highly favorable mail that we got in response helped me to convince the president of NBC that the country was indeed receptive to the idea of blacks in a more acceptable role.

TWT: Of all the sitcoms that you have been involved with, which was your favorite?

SL: *The Dick Van Dyke Show* was my second favorite. My favorite was a show that only lasted one season. It was called *My World and Welcome to It*. It was based on the writings of James Thurber, and it won the Emmy award as the best new comedy of the year—and it was cancelled at the end of its first year. It was a relatively sophisticated show, but the only time slot that was available was 7:30 PM Monday nights as a lead in to *Laugh In*. It was a totally inappropriate time slot and couldn't survive.

TWT: In your career, what have you enjoyed doing the most or found the most rewarding?

SL: Acting. It is the most rewarding, and you get the most appreciation for your acting. Acting is best for your ego, producing is best for your bank balance, and directing is best for your feeling of creativity and being able to make something out of nothing.

TWT: How are you and the other partners of CALVADA Productions compensated for the airing of *The Dick Van Dyke Show*?

SL: It's all part of the negotiation. Nick-at-Nite, or any other entity for that matter, must negotiate the terms with our agent at The William Morris Agency. The William Morris Agency then collects any revenues due by the terms of the contract and distributes it to the appropriate parties. Both the number of times the show will air as well as the duration of the contract affect the negotiated price.

TWT: What is the most memorable moment of your show business career?

SL: There have been so many it is difficult for me to pick just one. When I was on Broadway as an actor, my life was peppered with highlights. A successful opening night on Broadway is one of the most exciting experiences you can have. I had several such successful openings.

TWT: What do you think of today's television shows?

SL: I'm not really very equipped to answer that. For the most part, I don't like it. It's the kind of television that's relatively easy to do. What they are doing for the most part is to surround a central character with a lot of eccentrics. That is not to say that I haven't done it in my past. On *The Andy Griffith Show* I used Don Knotts and Jim Nabors as funny, humor creating characters, but I find more satisfaction in shows where you present an idea or state a philosophy and build your show on values rather than characters.

TWT: Can you explain to us how the "multiple camera method" was used?

SL: That innovation was promoted by Desi Arnaz. At the time, live television was using multiple cameras because they cut the show right on the air (camera 1 close up vs. camera 2 long shots, etc.). He decided that the technique could be applied to film and, thus, enable you to film a show in front of a live audience and play it in continuity. Of course, he used it first for *I Love Lucy* and was able to get authentic laugh responses instead of laugh responses out of a laugh machine. *The Danny Thomas Show* was the next show to use the technique, and I was the second director in Hollywood to learn the technique and apply it. From that point on, I used it on several of my other shows—*The Dick Van Dyke Show; Good Morning, World; Hey, Landlord;* and quite a few others.

TWT: Then you actually ended up with three reels of film.

SL: Yes, and the editor can select the angle he wants for any particular sequence. A single audio track accompanies each of the angles.

TWT: Please tell us about your family.

SL: My wife is still living after sixty-four years. I have a son who lives in Santa Fe, New Mexico, and he has two daughters. He is an Investment Banker. I have a daughter who has two grown up sons, and she lives in Idaho. She is a psychiatric social worker.

TWT: What is a typical day like for you nowadays?

SL: I wrote a book called *And the Show Goes On,* and it won considerable acceptance. I am currently writing a second book about my adventures traveling in the making of *I Spy.* I put in about two to four hours a day in front of the computer. Then I go to the golf range and hit balls for an hour or two. Then I return home to write letters, read, etc.

TWT: Can you give us your assessment of *The Dick Van Dyke Show* cast?

SL: By now, the television viewing public has come to recognize that this was an exceptional group of talent. Mary Tyler Moore was quite special, and Dick Van Dyke was unique, and Carl Reiner was a very talented creator of material. It was as good an example of on air chemistry as you are ever likely to find. I would not do a sitcom today. The talent pool is not nearly as deep as it was when I was putting *The Dick Van Dyke Show* together.

TWT: How are you most well known from your fans' perspective?

SL: Mostly by my career in pictures. Old pictures never die. They refer to my work in *Guys and Dolls* and *Tortilla Flat* and *It's a Wonderful Life*.

TWT: What software do you enjoy using on your computer?

SL: Of course, Windows is very important. There is a chess game that I enjoy playing. And I am very dependent on the reference materials (thesaurus, atlases, etc.). I also have America Online, but I really don't know how to use it!

TWT: Do you remain in good health today?

SL: I think so, and so does my doctor. Until something tells me otherwise, I will agree with him.

Leonard spoke with amazing eloquence. His command of the English language was nothing less than outstanding. It was almost impossible to believe that the words he used could flow so easily from one's mouth. This was one huge television icon! What a privilege for me to be able to interview him and have him share his insights.

As I prepared for my first excursion to California in January of 1997, I sent Sheldon another letter asking if he might consider meeting me during my upcoming visit. I did not receive a reply. Little did I know at that time that Sheldon's health had been rapidly deteriorating, and he was suffering from what turned out to be a fatal infection around his heart. Sheldon died on January 11, 1997, while I was in Los Angeles during my first *Dick Van Dyke Show*-related trip.

As a 1929 graduate of Syracuse University, Sheldon was often invited back to be a featured guest speaker at the University to offer his perspectives on the communications and television industry. Sheldon had done it all. His career spanned nearly seven decades, and his credits were staggering.

Perhaps Sheldon's greatest ability was his unique sense of knowing what would work in a storyline and what would not. Yet his manner was such that his opinions were always presented as suggestions, not demands. And in hindsight, cast and crew always appreciated his impact, realizing that their show's success was largely attributable to Sheldon's guidance and direction.

The vast wealth of knowledge and years of experience shared by Leonard were immeasurable. Sheldon is probably remembered mostly by his associates and colleagues as "teacher." Further, his willingness to mentor is confirmed by countless numbers of current day actors, producers, and directors who have achieved their own success—all "Sheldon Leonard" productions.

The next time you're tuned to TV Land, take a glance at the ending credits, and, undoubtedly, you'll see that Sheldon Leonard was involved in some capacity. "Classic television" from one "classy" guy.

# 6

## *Earle Hagen*

My initial contact with Earle Hagen was by snail mail. I had sent Earle several questions, and he responded to me pretty quickly with a very nice letter.

I was especially interested in getting in touch with Earle, not only because of his involvement with *The Dick Van Dyke Show* but also because of my personal interest in music composition and arranging. Music has always played a major role in my life, and I have been a singer and performer with various musical groups ever since I was a teenager.

Earle is a musical genius, and his list of credits is absolutely staggering. You might not recognize his face or even his name, but you can certainly identify his musical compositions in an instant.

Earle can proudly take credit for some of the most recognizable TV theme songs of all time. Included in his extensive list of compositions is *The Dick Van Dyke Show* theme and the well known finger snapping, foot tapping, guitar strumming tune from *The Andy Griffith Show*. He can also be related to the fabulous themes from *Gomer Pyle*, *That Girl*, *Mod Squad*, and *I Spy*, just to name a few more.

Our initial contact by mail turned into a friendship via email and an eventual telephone interview with Earle from his home in the California desert.

TWT: Can you tell us how you got started in the field of music?

EH: I studied music in high school and played the trombone. When I was eighteen, I was on the road playing music. In 1941, I enlisted into a radio production unit in Santa Ana, California. I got more interested in writing than playing and just did writing the three and a half years that I was in the service. I also studied with Ernest Toch and began to get serious about writing. When I got out of the service, I was a houseman for a couple of record companies. Eventually Alfred Neumann offered me a contract at Fox, and I spent seven years there. When the studio started to close down, Herbie Spencer and I decided we would go into partnership. The William Morris Agency had three pilots they needed music for: *The Danny Thomas Show*, *The Ray Bolger Show*, and *Celeste Holm*. Two out of the three sold, and we were in television. About the time that *The Andy Griffith Show* came along, we were doing a show called *My Sister Eileen* at Columbia. Herb decided he wanted to stay with Lou Edelman, and I decided I'd go with Sheldon. I stayed with Sheldon for the better part of his career.

TWT: *The Andy Griffith Show* was a spin off from *The Danny Thomas Show*, right?

EH: Yes. The town was busy with pilots, and the first one that really hit hard was *Griffith*. And then from *Griffith* came *Gomer* and eventually *Mayberry RFD*, and then Marlo started her show. One way or another, I wound up kind of being the "house man" for Danny Thomas and Sheldon.

TWT: How long did it take you to write the theme from the *Griffith* show?

EH: I was in partnership with Herbie Spencer at the time. We had a whole summer to come up with something, but neither of us had any ideas. Then one morning I got up and I thought, you know, this thing ought to be simple enough to whistle. In the end, it took me about an hour to write it. I called my drummer and bass and guitar player, and I rented a little studio on Fairfax Avenue, and I went in, and I made a demo to main title length. The next day I went by Sheldon's and played him the demo. He liked it and made plans to shoot Andy and Ronnie walking alongside the lake with a couple of fishing rods over their shoulders. And that was it. That was as hard as it was. It took a long time to get simplified enough to do something like that.

TWT: Is it true that you whistled *The Andy Griffith Show* theme on the recording?

EH: Yes, it's true. I had never whistled before, and I've never whistled since. A guitar player and whistler named Muzzy Marcellano called me up and said, "If you do that again I'll break your lips." But anyway, it caught and stayed on pretty well.

TWT: The next show was *Van Dyke*?

EH: Yes, after *Griffith* came *Van Dyke*. When we did the pilot for *Van Dyke*, for some reason or other I just felt like it would be better to go with the big band sound. I made a demo of the theme and played it for Carl, and Carl loved it. I had that little flip in the music, and he shot two versions of the opening—one where Dick tripped over the ottoman and one where he didn't.

TWT: Can you comment on the very first version of *The Dick Van Dyke Show* theme?

EH: Well, it had bongos! But that didn't hang around for too long. As a matter of fact, I don't even remember that version. I had a friend of mine ask "Do you remember the version you did with the bongos?" and I said, "Get outta here."

TWT: What do you think is your most recognizable theme song?

EH: I think *Griffith* by far. *Griffith* has become a piece of Americana. If you go into Nashville for a recording session, in between takes the guys will start faking on the *Andy Griffith* theme. Andy can't go anywhere without somebody whistling at him. I think it's probably one of the ten top recognizable themes in television. And I'm not sure what the other nine are. *Mission Impossible*, probably. But I think *Van Dyke* is up there pretty well, too.

TWT: Can you explain how it worked for musical numbers that were performed on the show?

EH: This was generally the only time I was really involved in the production aspect of the show. We would prerecord the music in the studio, and the cast would lip sync to the recording.

TWT: So were you actually on the set the night the show was filmed?

EH: Yes, but let me explain how it would work. After an episode was edited into final form, I'd break it down and write the music. On the next shooting day, I'd generally come in at 6:00 with the band, and we would record the music for the show that I had recently broken down. I'd score the bridges and cues and just do it to stopwatch. By that time, it was ready for that night's show to start, so I'd put the band on the stage. We always did "play ons" and "play offs," and we introduced the cast. In between takes, we'd play dance music or something to keep it alive. And if there was a number onstage that required live music, we would do it. We were usually done by 9:00 and would go home.

TWT: How much of the music that you wrote do you own?

EH: I own the thematic rights in conjunction with the company. Revenue in the form of recording, sheet music, and college music are split 50/50 with the production company. But then I also negotiated for the background rights. In those days they were worthless, but I figured one day they'd be worth something, and, at the same time, we were providing them with a lot of services that they basically weren't paying a lot of money for. We gave a lot of service, and that was the perk that we got in return for the service. And in essence, I became a music department.

TWT: How does it work now when *The Dick Van Dyke Show* theme or another theme gets played on the air? Do you get performance royalties?

EH: Yes, I get performance royalties from BMI.

TWT: I recall hearing *The Dick Van Dyke Show* theme during a Tropicana commercial.

EH: Yes, I licensed that during the Super Bowl a few years ago. That was nice. I wish we had a lot of those.

TWT: Many times we saw live bands on the show like in "The Secret Life of Buddy and Sally" and "Big Max Calvada." Were you part of these groups, and/or did you conduct them?

EH: Yes, I was a part of these groups. If there was a band in the scene, it was my band, and I conducted it. I was also seen on *The Danny Thomas Show* because, whenever we had a nightclub scene, the band was usually the background of the set, and I would conduct live on screen.

TWT: Did you compose any of the many production numbers which were performed on the show?

EH: No, I didn't. Most of the numbers that we used were standards. However, I usually arranged them for use on the show.

TWT: What was the process that you used to come up with background music?

EH: Every show I ever did was scored, and I treated every show as a separate piece. There are some really nice moments in the *Griffith Show* between Andy and Ron Howard, and they always lent themselves very nicely for scoring. There was more music on the *Griffith Show* than you would imagine. It was just nice in the background. There wasn't a lot on the *Van Dyke Show* because the show was very tight, and it was a comedy show, pure and simple.

TWT: How did you find time to do four or five shows all at the same time?

EH: You know, I really don't know how I did it. I did have help from such guys as Carl Brandt, J.J. Johnson, and Hugo Friedhofer. But by the same token, I had to break five shows down a week and then conduct them. It was sixteen hour days, seven days a week. Every single one of them was an attempt at new material.

TWT: When you watch a television show, are you distracted or impacted by the underlying score?

EH: It does affect me. I can't divorce myself from the fact that I was one of the constructionists in the process, and I'm as interested in the construction as I am in the process. If music tips the scene to me or if it tries to be funny, if it doesn't heighten the emotional stakes, those things call my attention. And I've gotten to the point now where I can't watch episodic television. I don't care whether the guy was in wardrobe or whether he was a makeup artist, whether he was a musician or a player or a writer, when we were doing these shows, everyone cared about their contribution to the process. Now it's like there isn't anybody from the entertainment business making the decisions as to what's entertainment.

TWT: Do you still have all of the scores that you wrote for all of the shows?

EH: I donated all of the early works (*Griffith, Van Dyke, That Girl*) to the University of Wyoming. The music from *I Spy* and from there on was donated to UCLA's archives. The archives at UCLA are really unbelievable. They have a ton of people there, and, if you need something, they'll make you a CD or tape and provide research material for students.

TWT: Do you still write music nowadays?

EH: No, I don't. I put it away. I spent fifty-two years at it. And I finally just got to the point where the business was changing. I just decided that I got tired of repeating myself. Anybody that tells you they can do three-thousand television shows without repeating themselves is crazy. And it was time, so I put it down.

TWT: What was the last project you did before you retired?

EH: In 1986, I returned to *Mayberry* to do an *Andy Griffith Show* made for TV movie. It was a great time and wonderful to work with everyone from the show again. And before you ask, yes, I did whistle the theme one more time for the movie. It was just as out of tune then as it was for the original!

TWT: Do you have a favorite *Dick Van Dyke Show* episode?

EH: Although I cannot remember a bad show in the five years we were on the air, my favorite show was when they were waiting for Laura to have her baby.

TWT: How would you summarize your overall experience working on *The Dick Van Dyke Show*?

EH: *The Dick Van Dyke Show* had a great "Sheldon Leonard" cast. Leonard put together an ensemble group who reacted to the challenge of comedy with professionalism and talent. The entire show was a great experience.

My September 2002 trip to LA also included a journey to the desert and a wonderful visit with Earle Hagen.

Earle graciously welcomed me into his home, and we sat and enjoyed a cup of coffee at the kitchen table while he shared his memories of the music and television business. It was just intriguing!

Earle described the very unique relationship that he had with Sheldon Leonard. Sheldon and Earle were longtime associates both professionally and personally, and Earle had wonderful stories to tell about their many fishing excursions together. Earle and Sheldon, along with their wives, also traveled the world over together as the two searched for just the right shooting locations for *I Spy*.

He took special pleasure in pointing out a photo of Sheldon which hangs proudly on his study wall. On the photo is an inscription written by Sheldon: "To Earle—Of your many talents, your talent for friendship is the most valued." It's very obvious that Earle and Sheldon were true comrades.

Earle's home and office are further adorned with his Emmy and many other music awards, photos of Leonard, Cosby, Culp, and Griffith, his film scoring books, and more. There are also many photos of his beloved wife of nearly sixty years, Lou, who passed away in February 2003. As one peruses the collection of personal memorabilia, it is overwhelmingly evident that Earle's musical contributions have made an indelible mark on the enduring history of so many classic television shows.

We hopped into Earle's golf cart for the short ride to the country club where he treated me to brunch. After we finished eating, Earle gave me a tour of the clubhouse—including one of the main rooms which had been named the "Earle Hagen room" in honor of Earle. Earle noted that he finds pleasure in scheduling jazz groups to come and perform in the "Earle Hagen" room at the Country Club each Monday night during the season.

We returned to Earle's home for more entertaining conversations and stories of Earle's adventures in the music business. Although I sat in awe of this musical legend, I felt as though Earle and I had made a genuine connection.

During a visit to Palm Springs in January 2005, Earle invited me to join him for dinner and entertainment in the "Earle Hagen" room at the country club. We had a delightful time catching up over cocktails, magnificent food, delicious desserts, and the marvelous musical performance of vibraphonist, Peter Appleyard. What a memory it created—a remarkable evening of good times with a good friend. Our unique association continues today.

# 7

## *Dick Van Dyke*

Of course the ultimate goal for a fan and publisher of a newsletter about *The Dick Van Dyke Show* would be to get the opportunity to interview the man himself. Right?

I had talked with Sol Leon, Dick's agent at The William Morris Agency, and Sol had referred me to Dick's publicist, a very nice guy by the name of Bob Palmer. I had talked with Bob a couple of times in the fall of 1995, and he indicated that it "looked good" for me to be able to do an interview with Dick—we just had to pin Dick down at some point and get it scheduled along with everything else that Dick had going on. Bob asked that I give him a call back in a couple of months.

Then, to my surprise, I got a call from Bob in December of 1995, with some exciting news. First, Bob wanted to let me know that Dick had received the first two issues and really liked the publication. Second, he wanted to tell me that Dick had referred to *The Walnut Times* in an interview he had done that day for a special program about the 50th anniversary of CBS. VERY cool! Since Dick had mentioned the newsletter, Bob had taken the opportunity to remind Dick that he had promised to do an interview with me. Bob suggested I give a call to him early in the new year and assured me he'd be doing all he could to help me out.

Due to Dick's demanding commitments shooting *Diagnosis Murder*, there was not time until the end of the season in April, 1996 to schedule the interview. Bob gave a call to advise that Dick would be phoning me later that morning to finally do the long-awaited interview. I have to admit that it was very weird to answer the phone and have the person on the other end of the line be Dick Van Dyke. It seemed even odder when Dick asked to speak to Mr. Van Deusen.

We exchanged pleasantries and started the interview.

TWT: Are you surprised at the continuing popularity of *The Dick Van Dyke Show*?

DVD: Yes, I am. It's been over thirty years. Who would have ever thought that it would still be around? I am really amazed that we are on our third generation. I went to Phoenix recently to visit my grandchild's school for "Reading Week." I couldn't believe the six and seven year olds with a piece of paper and a pencil who wanted my autograph! I was surprised they knew who I was at all. It really was a thrill.

TWT: Could you comment on the roles that Carl Reiner and Sheldon Leonard played in the show's success.

DVD: Sheldon was the very beginning of three camera sitcoms, and he knew his storylines and construction better than anybody. He and Carl used to go at it pretty good in some friendly arguments about what you could and could not do. I learned a lot from them. Carl is a genius, that's all, and the nicest human being I have ever met. He had some very fresh ideas and wanted to break the mold a bit.

TWT: Is it true that the show was the beginning of what were and are deeply rooted friendships?

DVD: Yes, that's true. It was like breaking up a family when we ended the show.

TWT: We've been in touch with Frank Adamo regarding his role on the show. Frank noted that "working on *The Dick Van Dyke Show* with Dick was one of the great joys of my life and one that gave me the opportunity to work with some very wonderful and gifted people. Thank you, Dick."

DVD: Frank started out with me as my dresser in the theatre in New York when I did *Bye Bye Birdie*. I told him I was going to California and asked if he wanted to come. He was with me for all the years of *The Dick Van Dyke Show*. When Mary started her series, he went with her, so he's been involved with us for a long, long time. He's a remarkable guy.

TWT: What in your opinion is the most classic moment from *The Dick Van Dyke Show*?

DVD: I kind of judge shows by how much fun I had doing them rather than how they look on the air. My favorite was "Where Did I Come From?" We had a ball doing that show. We changed it every five minutes every time we thought of a new joke or a new gag. I think it was still in progress when we filmed it. Everyone had a wonderful time on that show.

TWT: We know from the showing of *The Chairman's Choice* what your favorite *Dick Van Dyke Show* episodes are. Do you have a least favorite?

DVD: There was one where a young guy was a bullfighter. I thought that one was very weak. There were a couple of others although, right now, I can't think of them. I think we only threw out one script. We really prided ourselves on being able to fix a script and make it work. By and large, I think our average was pretty good.

TWT: How many permanent sets were there on the show?

DVD: All the sets were lined up in a row on one big stage in front of the audience. Three cameras covered the actions, and when we changed scenes, the cameras would roll down the line to the next set. The only permanent ones were our bedroom/living room/kitchen and the writer's office. And then we had space for sets we would build as we needed them.

TWT: I believe these sets were recreated for *The Dick Van Dyke Show* retrospective program.

DVD: Yes, they were. And they did a pretty good job. They found the plans for the sets and also looked at some footage. Of course, who knew how it looked in color, because it was black and white.

TWT: Is there any truth to the fact that particular colors were chosen because of the way they would appear in black and white?

DVD: Now that's a question I can't answer. There were no bright colors, they were all muted colors.

TWT: Did you keep any outtakes or bloopers from the show like they do nowadays?

DVD: They did keep those back then because they used to make a reel, and, at the end of the shooting season, we would have our wrap party, and they would show the footage. There was nothing particularly crazy, just people blowing lines.

TWT: Fans are eternally hopeful that there will be a true reunion of the cast. Is there any possibility this might happen?

DVD: For some reason, there is resistance all around. Mary doesn't want to do it, and we're all so much older and everything. Carl agreed to the retrospective which he thought was a good idea, but trying to recreate the old show with a bunch of old geezers…(laughs)…how could we improve on it?

TWT: Have you ever been approached to reprise your role as Rob Petrie?

DVD: No, I never have.

TWT: If approached, would you consider it?

DVD: It would all depend on what the script was. I did get a call from John Laroquette. He wanted me to come and play his father.

TWT: As the Chairman of Nick-at-Nite, do you have much control over what they show of you, or how they use your voice overdubs?

DVD: No. It's really an honorary title. I'm not really chairman of anything. They call me the chairman, but I don't make any decisions.

TWT: Can we expect to see *The Dick Van Dyke Show* on Nick-at-Nite for some time to come?

DVD: Yes, they just picked us up for another three years.

TWT: Do you have any memorabilia from the show…say for instance, the Mel Cooley punching bag?

DVD: No. I don't have any of that stuff. I drew that caricature on there of Mel, and I'd love to have it. I don't know what happened to those things. I do have quite a few pictures.

TWT: No heads of lettuce?

DVD: (Laughs) No, no heads of lettuce.

TWT: We have seen you use both your right and left hands to draw and write. Are you right-handed or left-handed? Do you have two autographs?

DVD: Actually, I'm a little screwed up. I write with my right hand, but I draw with my left. Isn't that awful? I don't know which side of my brain to use.

TWT: Will *Diagnosis Murder* be returning this fall?

DVD: They are after us to do it again. Of course, my main joy is working with my son, Barry.

TWT: We have noticed that the show has a lot of location shoots in Malibu. Is that to save you some travel time?

DVD: Yes, isn't that neat? We shoot right inside a beach front home. It's a nice big house. I'd like to have it!

TWT: What is your shooting schedule like?

DVD: The schedule is quite demanding. It takes seven days to shoot an hour episode. To be honest, I really don't like working without an audience because it's really not performing. I need an audience to tell me how I'm doing.

TWT: We understand you're quite a computer enthusiast.

DVD: I love computer graphics. I have the machine that they use on *SeaQuest* and *Deep Space Nine*. I can turn out wonderful animations and special effects. It's just great! I have a hobby room out over my garage with a blue screen. I photograph myself against the blue screen and then introduce myself into other footage. Remember "Never Bathe on Saturday" where I break the bathroom door down? When I come back out into the main room, it was me "now" instead of me "then!"

TWT: Being a computer fan, do you subscribe to any online services?

DVD: No, I'm not online at all.

TWT: Can you tell us about your family?

DVD: My children have all turned out to be wonderful parents. I have four children and seven grandchildren. Barry has four children, one of which was on an episode of *Diagnosis Murder*. My son, Chris, is in Hong Kong and the second in command at Nike. My two daughters are in Scottsdale, Arizona.

TWT: With all of the awards you have received, what do you consider your greatest accomplishment?

DVD: I think the Television Hall of Fame. I was able to celebrate the evening and award with Barry and my two daughters and two of my grandkids. They did a terrible thing with the television broadcast, though. I had my acceptance speech and thanked all of the people who I felt I needed to thank, and they cut it all down to nothing. Everyone must think I forgot about them. I would love to get my hands on the original footage, so I could send copies to my friends.

TWT: How would *The Dick Van Dyke Show* be different if it were done today?

DVD: I often wish we had the latitude back then that they have today. There were many subject matters that we couldn't even touch back then. Carl would have done it well and in very good taste, and I think we would have handled them better than anybody.

As I wrapped up the interview, I asked Dick if I could send him a couple of items to sign for me.

"Sure, send them out," Dick said, "and I'll sign them and get them back to you."

I thanked Dick for his time, and he kidded me about how long it had taken to finally get the interview done. But it had finally happened, and, from my perspective, it was awesome.

I packaged up some photos and a pair of *Dick Van Dyke Show* related baseball caps I had acquired and sent them out for Dick to autograph.

A couple of weeks later, a package arrived back on my doorstep with a Malibu return address, and I knew instantly from where it had come.

As I removed the items from the box, the inscription on one of the hats immediately caught my eye.

"To David, The Head Walnut," Dick wrote. "God Bless, Dick Van Dyke."

Dick had dubbed me the "Head Walnut"—an identifier which I have subsequently used in the newsletter. Instead of the original "From the Editor" column, it was transformed into the "From the Head Walnut" column, along with a caricature graphic to match. I also have used the nickname ever since as my email address—headwalnut@thewalnuttimes.com!

The first stop on my January 1997 trip to Los Angeles was to the set of *Diagnosis Murder*. As I got up that morning at 4 AM to get ready, I turned on the portable television in the bedroom to provide some dim light.

Ironically, I turned on Nick at Nite and *The Dick Van Dyke Show* was just starting. I had a funny feeling as it seemed somewhat strange to know that in another few hours that I would finally be meeting the man that I was watching on television!

Jack and I arrived to a gray, dismal, rainy day. In fact, it was pouring rain. Having escaped the cold winter temperatures of the Northeast, the one thing we hoped for was sunny, warm temperatures. But they were nowhere in sight!

We arrived on the set and were escorted to a large open area—kind of like a warehouse, with many tables set up. Much of the cast and crew were eating lunch.

We stood off to the side while the escort approached Bob Palmer to give him my name. Bob reacted immediately, having arranged for the visit. He was expecting us.

Interestingly, Bob had just been chatting with Sol Leon, Dick's agent of many years from The William Morris Agency.

Bob introduced Jack and me to Sol. Actually, I had also talked with Sol on a few different occasions in the past, and it was nice to meet him.

Bob advised us that Dick was in his trailer and would return to the set in a little while. While we were waiting, Bob gave us a tour of the hospital set which was housed at this location. It was very interesting to get a close look in person at what we had only previously seen in various *Diagnosis Murder* episodes.

Shooting was about to resume, and Bob gave us instructions as to where to stand so we could see what was going on but still be out of the way.

As we waited for the scene to begin, we heard that familiar voice as he was coming down the hallway toward us. There he was in person—Dick Van Dyke!

Bob approached a woman several feet away who was next to Dick and spoke quietly to her. The lady was Barbara Peterson, Dick's wardrobe assistant. As Bob talked to her, she glanced in our direction and noted our presence, perched up against the wall. She smiled and then returned her attention to Dick and the scene that was being rehearsed.

Bob came back across the room towards me. "Barbara will introduce you to Dick after they complete the next scene."

The scene was rehearsed and then shot for the cameras. The director yelled cut, and the cast and crew began to scatter.

Barbara looked our way and gave a motion to Dick. They came toward us.

"Dick," she said, "This is David Van Deusen, the publisher of *The Walnut Times*." Dick reached out to shake my hand.

"Dick Van Dyke," I said, as I shook his hand. "It is great to finally meet you."

With that brief introduction complete, Bob suggested that we pull up a couple of chairs so we could sit down and talk for awhile during the break.

Jack began to take photos and shoot some video while Dick, Bob, Barbara, and I all talked about the newsletter, how it began, and what my future issues would include.

Dick asked about what else Jack and I were planning to do during our visit and commented that he hoped the torrential rain would subside. "If this weather keeps up," Dick joked, "I'm moving to California!"

I explained that we hoped to meet up with Rose Marie, Ann Guilbert, and Julie Paris, Jerry's daughter.

"Sounds like you're going to be busy," said Dick. "Are you going to see any of the sights while you're here?"

"We're going to try to go to Disneyland," I replied.

"Go on me," said Dick.

"Go on you?" I questioned.

"Sure," Dick continued. "I have a lifetime Gold Pass for all my work with Disney. Just let me know when you want to go and I'll give a call down there. There will be tickets waiting for you."

"That's great! Thanks a lot," I replied, as Jack and I shared a big smile between each other.

We watched several more scenes during our set visit. It was very interesting to observe the process.

Jack and Dick Van Dyke

I had told Dick that I was going to be bringing the "giant" walnut so we could take a few photos. During one of the breaks in the shooting, Dick came over and asked about the walnut. I pulled it out of my bag and handed it to him. Dick thought it was great, and we laughed about the huge particle of absorbitron that would have been inside a walnut of this size! Jack took some marvelous pictures during our visit, including the one of Dick and me with the giant walnut and "no thumbs" which is the photo on the front cover.

Our time on the set had been fabulous, and Dick (and Barbara and Bob) had been just wonderful to us. We appreciated the fact that we had been given the chance to even get on the set. We thanked everyone for having us and turned to head for the exit.

"Make sure you let me know what day you want to go to Disney," Dick said.

As we headed to the car, I stopped to reflect on what had just transpired. Somehow I had gone from being a newsletter publisher about *The Dick Van Dyke Show* to meeting Dick on the set of his television show! Wow! My first in-person meeting with Dick Van Dyke had been terrific and one I will always remember! And, to top it all off, two days later, Jack and I were guests of Dick Van Dyke at Disneyland. Fantastic!

February 1999 marked my second visit to the set of *Diagnosis Murder*. Fred and I arrived around noon. Bob Palmer was there again to help facilitate our visit and invited Fred and me to join him for lunch.

After lunch, we watched several scenes being filmed and had the opportunity to talk with Dick and Barry Van Dyke during breaks in the shooting.

"When we're done here, we'll go out back to my trailer so we can talk," said Dick.

As the final scenes of the day were being rehearsed and shot, I grabbed my video camera from my bag and took the opportunity to grab some behind-the-scenes footage for the archives. They are a lot of fun to watch every now and then as they encapsulate Dick's attitude and demeanor for the laid back and relaxed shooting atmosphere. Dick was always singing or doing a little dancing during the breaks.

Shooting wrapped for the day and we headed out the rear of set to Dick's trailer in the parking lot. As we entered the main living area, something caught my eye. Dick had a great photo of Stan Laurel (Dick's idol) and Oliver Hardy hanging on the trailer wall. The photo clearly defined the atmosphere for the trailer.

"What would you like to do?" Dick asked. "Do you want to take some photos?"

"Do you know that *The Dick Van Dyke Show* theme song has words?" I inquired.

"Absolutely," said Dick. "Morey wrote them."

"Yes," I replied, as I pulled a copy of the sheet music Morey had sent me out of my folder. "Would you indulge me and sing it with me while Fred records us?"

"Sure," said Dick. And so we sang it together. It's a classic piece of footage that's a special part of my *Dick Van Dyke Show* archives.

"I'm trying to form a barbershop quartet," explained Dick, "but I'm not getting any response to the ad I put in my local paper. I've always loved to sing, and we recently incorporated a barbershop number into an episode of *Diagnosis Murder*. It was a lot of fun!"

We took a few photos, and then I asked Dick if he would record an audio promo for me for the newsletter to use on my website.

Again, Dick was as gracious as ever and agreed to read the short piece that I had written. When he finished the take, Fred confirmed that he had gotten it on tape, and we were all set.

"I can do it better than that," said Dick. "Let's do it again!"

And so, Dick performed it a couple more times—until he was happy with the result. Of course, I was thrilled to have a promo for my publication. You can still hear it today on my website.

At this point, I need to mention and recognize Doug Denoff, son of writer/producer Sam Denoff, for all of his assistance with my website. A supporter of my efforts from the very start, Doug registered *The Walnut Times* domain name for me and has continued to renew the domain whenever its expiration approaches. Doug has also provided the web hosting to me free of charge since the website's creation—a very nice gesture on his part, and another terrific association solely due to walnuts!

My last visit to the set of *Diagnosis Murder* was in July, 2000 when Dick and I met to do the interview for the "Walnut" video. This is captured in detail in Chapter 13.

December of 2000 marked Dick's 75$^{th}$ birthday, and I wanted to send him a birthday/thank you gift for all of his support of the newsletter. But what kind of gift do you get for someone like Dick Van Dyke?

I recalled our conversation about Dick's desire to form a barbershop quartet and the fun we had singing the theme together. And then it hit me! What if I gave Dick a barbershop quartet arrangement of *The Dick Van Dyke Show* theme?

I should explain that, in the time between my 1999 visit and December of 2000, Dick had sung from time to time with an established barbershop quartet. In fact, he was honored by the SPEBSQSA organization in July 1999 as a Lifetime Member.

As I noted earlier, music composition and choral arranging has always been one of my other interests, yet I had never done a barbershop quartet arrangement before. Barbershop arrangements are very distinctive, and the style is strictly defined.

To get me started, the first thing I did was to order a barbershop quartet arranging manual from the Barbershop Quartet Society of America so I had a reference guide to assist me.

My next task was to contact Earle Hagen and request his permission to write such an arrangement.

I sent Earle an email and explained what I wanted to do for Dick for his birthday. Earle thought it was a great idea and gave me his go ahead to proceed. His only requirement was that I send him a copy of the finished arrangement so that he could see what I did with the song.

I worked and reworked the arrangement in the couple of months immediately preceding Dick's birthday until I was finally satisfied with the result. I sent it off to Earle for his review and awaited his feedback.

Earle's response? "The arrangement is outstanding," wrote Earle. Wow! What a compliment from this musical legend. I still have Earle's email in my archives.

I sent off a letter to Dick along with the arrangement to say thanks and wish him Happy Birthday. Soon after, I received an email from Dick which read as follows:

"Hi David! What a thoughtful gift! A stroke of genius, actually. I couldn't have thought of a better idea. It came today and I can't wait to get the quartet together to try it out. We'll sing it on my birthday and drink a toast to you!"

There's still more to come about this choral arrangement. Stay tuned!

Dick has been an ardent supporter of *The Walnut Times* from the very beginning of the publication. He has allowed his photo to be used under many circumstances, given permission for his drawings to be used, and has approved various other caricatures of himself for use in the newsletter. He enthusiastically participated in my walnut documentary (see Chapter 13), and has always made himself available to me when I've been visiting Los Angeles. We have certainly established a very unique rapport.

On my most recent trip to Los Angeles, Dick and I got together at a quaint café near his home in Malibu—a nice, casual lunch outing between a couple of friends.

And while Dick is surely a giant in the entertainment industry, I can also tell you that he's one of the more friendly, unassuming, and genuinely nice people you'll ever meet—a true gentleman.

Thank you, Dick, for your continued endorsement and unwavering support of my endeavor. You're the best!

# 8

## *Carl Reiner*

I felt very fortunate to have had the opportunity to interview so many of the cast at this stage of the life of the newsletter—Rose Marie, Morey Amsterdam, Ann Guilbert, Sheldon Leonard, and, most recently, Dick Van Dyke. Wow! I never could have imagined that this would have been possible.

I continued in my diligent and persistent pursuit of an interview with Carl Reiner, the creator, producer, and mastermind behind *The Dick Van Dyke Show*.

I spoke often with Carl's assistant, Barbara Scher, in my attempts to try to get a time for an interview. Carl was so encumbered with several projects always ongoing at once, that it was very difficult to get an interview scheduled.

One day the call finally came. It was Barbara Scher letting me know that Carl had some time available and would be happy to talk with me. She proceeded to fill me in on how we would "get connected."

"Call this number precisely at this time," Scher instructed. "When they answer the phone, say the following exactly or they will hang up on you."

I realized the necessity for such details as I was sure that there were probably unsolicited calls made frequently to Mr. Reiner's house—and the people answering their phone needed a way to ensure that my telephone call was legitimate. At the same time, I felt as though I was involved in some type of subversive, underground activity. It was like some kind of secret code.

In any case, when the appointed hour arrived, I made the call as dictated, and the next thing I knew, Carl was on the other end of the line.

"Hi David," said Reiner. "I know we were supposed to talk now, but I just arrived home and would like to have some dinner and watch some of the Democratic convention. And I don't want to rush you. How about I call you later tonight, and I'll pay for the call? Would 11:00 PM your time be okay with you?"

I didn't care what time it would be as long as I got to talk with Carl.

"Sounds fine, Carl," I responded. "I'll talk with you later."

At about 11:05, the phone rang, and I answered, expecting it to be Carl on the other end. Sure enough, it was him.

"Hi, David," he began, "Carl Reiner calling." He continued. "I just woke someone else up in your town. I dialed your number wrong and got someone who had no idea who I wanted to talk to!"

"Did you tell them who you were?" I asked, thinking that the recipient of the erroneous call would have an interesting story to tell at work the next day.

"No," Carl replied. "I just hung up on them and redialed your number!"

And so, we were off to an entertaining beginning to the interview.

TWT: Do you still watch *The Dick Van Dyke Show* today? If so, how much do you remember about each of the shows?

CR: I do watch it from time to time. I don't always remember what is in a particular episode, but I do remember everything that we did.

TWT: You're considered a genius by your associates. How do you react to that comment?

CR: Well, I don't know if I'm a genius…but the show was about something I knew about. If you get one man's reality into a show, it usually works better. After a while, I got an awful lot of help from several wonderful writers…Belson and Marshall and Persky and Denoff. Persky and Denoff were my right hand men and eventually became my story editors.

TWT: Although you were a story consultant in later years and did not actually do the writing, did you still maintain control over the show?

CR: Every word that went out there was mine. The only time I lost a little control was in the last twelve shows when I went to do *The Russians are Coming*. That was the only time I was ever away. The show was my "baby," and, before I left, I had already written the last twelve scripts. Those are the only shows that I don't remember everything about because, as you do a show, you invent little things along the way. But for the most part, every word that was there went through the sieve.

TWT: Did you always come out and warm up the audience before a show?

CR: Yes, I did. Warming up an audience is a very strange thing. You warm them up by getting them happy. But you have to be careful that you don't tell bigger jokes than you have written for the show because then the show looks flat. Morey Amsterdam would always come out and tell a few jokes. And I would always have to warn him because he could tell jokes in front of the audience that we weren't allowed to air over the network. I never let him go on too long…it was a few jokes and out! We did not want to compete with the material the audience was going to see in a few minutes.

TWT: We recently discovered the footage of the cast in the Kent cigarette commercials. Can you share your perspective on this?

CR: We fought that for a little bit. We didn't like our stars doing that. I voted against it but couldn't win because the networks and sponsors had a big say in those days. I wouldn't have allowed it today. It sort of cheapens it when your star, who is supposed to be a real person, comes out and starts selling a product. They tried to integrate it into the characters of the show, and I didn't like it at all. The actors did it very well because they are wonderful performers, but I hated the idea of using our characters to sell products.

TWT: Why was the show so successful? Did you realize at the time that the show would become such a classic?

CR: I knew it was good, and I knew we had something very special the first year. I think it was successful because it had some reality to it. I based it on something I knew a lot about. It was about the working and home life of a guy who works on a variety show for television. And I had done that for several years previously with my involvement with Sid Caesar.

TWT: Do you think there has ever been a finer cast ensemble?

CR: As far as I'm concerned, there hasn't been a better cast that does that kind of thing. There are wonderful ensemble casts now. *Seinfeld* and *Friends* are just wonderfully cast and the chemistry is very obvious. But the foreground is the reason you tune into a show. You have to like the people. Then the cast has to produce stuff that you laugh at or like. Tim Allen and his cast members on *Home Improvement* are also very good. Their next door neighbor character that is hidden is kind of a "tip of the hat" to the *Van Dyke Show*, because I stayed hidden as Alan Brady for two years.

TWT: Two favorite episodes of fans of the show are "Never Bathe on Saturday" and "Coast-to-Coast Big Mouth."

CR: They are two of my favorites as well. Persky and Denoff wrote "Coast-to-Coast Big Mouth" and gave me my best role as Alan Brady. Until we started writing more complicated shows with Alan Brady in them, I had to turn him around. I turned around because those shows were written, and it would be unfair to the writing to not see Alan Brady's face. My conceit was originally that if they saw me in the first year, I had a history on television of being a "second banana" on the *Sid Caesar Show*. I didn't want somebody to say, "That's not a big star, that's only Carl Reiner". When we finally turned him around, we got some great shows watching this idiot beat up on his workers.

TWT: Was baldness a big issue back then in the entertainment business?

CR: Not with me. I was wearing a toupee on *The Show of Shows*. I wore a little one, and it got bigger and bigger as the years went on. My rule of thumb was that I never wore it for local events. Local television…I didn't wear it…National television…I wore it. I felt I was lying when I wore a toupee. Alan Brady was much more concerned about his bald head than I ever was.

TWT: Do you have a favorite *Dick Van Dyke Show* episode?

CR: I can't really pick one. It's like asking me who my favorite child is when I have three children. I would say that my favorite shows are the flashback type episodes…how they met, their life in the Army, the birth of the baby, the early times and the development of their relationship.

TWT: How involved were you in the casting of guest stars or bit players?

CR: Generally, we left those things to Ruth Burch, our casting director. But there were a raft of good character actors doing different shows on the lot. Many times we would think of a part that a friend could play, and then call them in. For instance, Phil Leeds was an old friend of mine who had his first comedy show on Dumont Television. I brought him in to play Blackey Sorrel, Buddy's pool shark brother. Phil is a wonderful guy, and you still see him on different shows every once and awhile.

TWT: What was it like to reprise the role of Alan Brady on *Mad About You*?

CR: Well, I had never done a situation comedy since *The Dick Van Dyke Show*. But Paul Reiser met me and said you've got to do the show. He said, "I don't want you, I want Alan Brady." That was the nicest thing he could have said. I wondered myself how he would sound today. I hadn't spoken as fast as that in a long time. It was very hard and it was kind of scary for a few minutes. Interestingly, the only changes I noticed in the way sitcoms are done today as compared to when we did *The Dick Van Dyke Show* is that each scene is done three times, and they pick the best one for the final take. We used to do it only once and then fix it later. The audience loves sitting there. They came to see how a TV show is made. It takes a little longer, going to one or two o'clock in the morning, when we used to be done by 9:30.

TWT: Will we ever see or hear from Laura and Rob Petrie again?

CR: You never say never. Of course, as we get older and older, we know what's happening. We're getting older and older! It has always been intriguing. Once for Dick's birthday party I couldn't attend because I had to go to a wedding in Texas. So as a gift, I wrote two sketches of what Rob and Laura and Buddy and Sally would be doing. They read them at the party and I won't tell you what they were about because that's private, but they were funny.

TWT: Do you have any personal memorabilia from the show?

CR: I have bound copies of all of the scripts with whatever notations we made.

TWT: Any toupees?

CR: The toupee I wore on the show was mine, but the others that I put on my head weren't. I still have some of them and give them away for charity events to be auctioned off. In fact, Dom Delouise bought one once.

TWT: Fans greatly enjoy the many production numbers done on the show.

CR: We loved to do production numbers and use the talents that the cast had. I especially liked them because a half hour show with production numbers meant I only had to write twenty minutes worth of script. Their three or four minutes of singing and dancing was like a relief. The wonderful thing about Dick and Mary is because they could both sing and dance, some of the dance numbers were perfected in four days while they were still rehearsing the rest of the show. Usually a good musical number took two weeks to prepare. It was really a credit to them that they looked that professional.

TWT: We understand that your wife, Estelle, is a singer.

CR: Estelle started singing late in life about twelve years ago. She's quite a jazz singer, but nobody knew it but me. She sings a lot of the black blues songs. She recently released her first CD entitled "Estelle Reiner" and sings a lot of great songs on it.

TWT: Do you have any hobbies?

CR: My work is my hobby. I used to play tennis until I did a benefit and tripped over a music stand and tore the tendons off my kneecaps. It took me nearly six months to get my leg back, but everything is fine now.

TWT: We understand you usually spend the summer months in France.

CR: Yes, I bought a small home in the south of France. Due to my commitments with the film I'm working on, we haven't been able to get over there, and it's killing us.

TWT: How have you been influenced by the computer revolution?

CR: I'm not "online," but the two books I've written I used WordPerfect on a laptop. I haven't written for about five months now. I'm hoping when I turn the computer back on, I'll remember how to do it all. I can't believe how much simpler it is to write on a computer, especially since I'm a bad typist. When we did *The Dick Van Dyke Show*, I did pages and pages—half with typewriter and half with pencil—there were Xs and scratch outs all over. Now it is a pleasure.

TWT: What do you feel is your greatest accomplishment in your career?

CR: The fact that I'm still working. And the fact that I have wonderful children who have given me three grandchildren. All in all, my greatest pleasure is writing, and writing *The Dick Van Dyke Show* was probably the highlight of my professional life.

Carl had been just tremendous. He had allowed me to conduct the interview at my own pace and ask as many questions as I wanted. Even better, he had provided great detail and tremendous insight into the creation and production of *The Dick Van Dyke Show*. I would have another great issue for subscribers!

I did not have an opportunity to meet Carl during my first excursion to Los Angeles in 1997, but I did manage to touch base with Barbara Scher before my 1999 trip to see if a meeting might be possible.

"Carl would like to meet you for lunch," she said. "There is a reservation for two at 2:00 PM in his name at the Chinese Restaurant on Little Santa Monica Boulevard in Beverly Hills. He'll see you then."

This is great, I thought. Lunch with Carl Reiner!

I arrived at the virtually empty restaurant about 1:50, announced myself, and was seated by the host at a small table for two in a side room. The best I could tell, there was not another patron in the entire restaurant.

Carl arrived precisely at 2:00 and was escorted to the table by the host. He quickly noticed that I had a lot of materials with me—a pad to take notes, some scripts, the giant walnut, and more.

He glanced around the room to observe that there was not another person in the place. Carl proceeded to ask the host if we could be moved to a larger table so there was more space for me to "spread out."

When his request was declined by the host who mumbled something about the possibility of other patrons possibly needing the larger table,

Carl returned a facial expression that I will never forget. I had all I could do to contain myself.

For all practical purposes, we had a private dining room for our lunch. And no other patron ever needed that larger table on the other side of the room!

Our conversation was terrific. Carl asked me more about the newsletter and how the whole endeavor got started. He was also interested in knowing what I really did for a living and inquired about my family and my other interests. I learned even more about Carl's family, and it turns out that his youngest son, Lucas, was born in 1960—just like me! I took notes as best I could, in between bites of food, in the small table space that was available.

One of the best stories was one that Carl told about a bet that Dick and he had made several years before about whether or not Dick would be bald by a certain age.

"Dick was absolutely insistent that he was losing his hair," Carl explained. "He was so sure that I bet him $500 that he would still have his hair—and I won. His hair is as thick now as it has ever been. It was all in fun, of course, and no money ever exchanged hands."

Carl continued. "My wife and I were recently over at Dick's home for dinner, and, shortly after we finished dinner, Dick excused himself from the table. When he returned, Dick surprised me with a check for $500 as payment of the bet made many years ago. We all had a good laugh. I initially thought I would frame the check but decided it could be put to much better use by one of Rob's children's charities. So, in the end, that's where the money ended up."

As our lunch drew to a close, I asked Carl if he would sign an original *Dick Van Dyke Show* script that I had been lucky enough to obtain.

"Sure," he said, as I slowly slid the script across the table toward him.

I tried to read what he was writing, but I couldn't make it out "upside down."

As he passed the script back to me he said, "You know, I think of you as the other DVD. Dick Van Dyke and David Van Deusen."

I looked down at the script to see the inscription: "For the other DVD, David Van Deusen, Love! Carl Reiner." Pretty nice.

Dick had previously dubbed me the "Head Walnut" and now Carl was referring to me as "the other DVD." I truly believed that I had somehow earned the respect of this brilliant, imaginative man. It was fantastic!

Carl and I saw each other again in the summer of 2000 when I was shooting the walnut documentary. All the details of that visit are contained in the specific chapter about the documentary.

Carl was busily working on two projects during my September, 2002, trip to Los Angeles, but Barbara Scher helped to facilitate setting up time for the two of us to meet. However, on the morning of the day that we were supposed to get together, Barbara called to advise that Carl's schedule had changed, and we would not be able to meet. I received the call on my way back from my visit with Earle Hagen in Rancho Mirage.

"Carl won't be able to meet with you this afternoon but would like very much to talk with you. Please give him a call when you get back to Los Angeles. He has a couple of things that he wants to tell you about."

DVD #5B (67) - Subtitle: "Very Old Shoes, Very Old Rice"

THE
    DICK
        VAN
            DYKE
                SHOW

WRITTEN BY
CARL REINER

*For the other D.V.D. David Van Deusen Too! — Carl Reiner*

Written:      August 2, 1963
Revised:      August 22, 1963
To be Filmed: August 27, 1963

The first thing that Carl told me all about was *The Alan Brady Show* animated program which was just beginning production. He was very impressed with the unique quality of the animation and the techniques that were being used. And he laughed as he recalled a part of his script which depicted a drawing of Rob, Buddy, and Sally and writing imprinted underneath that said "we love you Alan"—which had been crossed out in favor of "we like you Alan." Interestingly, the drawing used in the show was the original caricature drawing that Dick Van Dyke had done during the show's original run—and the one Dick gave me permission to use on *The Walnut Times* coffee mugs!

The second piece of information was about *The Dick Van Dyke Show* reunion script that he had started working on. I should note that TV Land has tried to take credit and state that the idea of a *Dick Van Dyke Show* Reunion came about at the 2003 TV Land Awards when Reiner mentioned the idea in his acceptance speech. But I can tell you that Carl had given me what he termed "the exclusive" information months earlier in our phone conversation in September of 2002.

I was simply astounded by Carl's comments when I requested that he reflect on the endurance *The Dick Van Dyke Show* as it celebrated its 40th anniversary. Carl wrote:

"Little did I dream that forty years after I created *The Dick Van Dyke Show*, that it would not only be seen in reruns but that there would be an actual newspaper that reports and comments on the doings and goings on of the show and its cast members."

Carl continued, "I have saved every copy of *The Walnut Times* and am seriously thinking of binding them into a book…and then again, I am seriously thinking of leaving them right where they are…on the shelf with all the scripts of *The Dick Van Dyke Show*. I never dreamed there would be a David Van Deusen in my life who would volunteer to take on this wonderful, wonderful project—the perpetuation of the myth of *The Dick Van Dyke Show*."

In my most recent trip to Los Angeles in January 2005, Carl invited me for lunch at one of his favorite Japanese restaurants in Beverly Hills.

As we entered the establishment, I mentioned to Carl that I had never been to a Japanese restaurant before. He stopped in his tracks and glanced at me with a gleam in his eye.

"A virgin!" he announced out loud to all of the patrons in the restaurant. "I've got a virgin!" We both chuckled at his remark as we sat down in a booth and he began to give me the rundown on sushi and other Japanese food. We proceeded to enjoy another wonderful lunch of delicious food and delightful conversation.

It is hard to express how extremely grateful I am to have had the opportunity to meet and become friends with Carl Reiner. He is truly an amazing individual. Carl was surely not obligated in any way to help me in my endeavor, yet the success of *The Walnut Times* is largely attributable to his personal endorsement and continued promotion of the publication. Carl has been an ardent supporter of *The Walnut Times* from the very start and has often referred to me as the "the archivist" of *The Dick Van Dyke Show*.

I offer my personal tip of the hat to Carl Reiner—the creative genius behind The *Dick Van Dyke Show* and a man who I am honored to call advocate, supporter, and friend.

Carl, giving "the eye" and having some fun with an absorbitron laden walnut

# 9

## *Mary Tyler Moore*

Unlike most of the cast members from *The Dick Van Dyke Show* who live in California, Mary Tyler Moore resides in New York State, maintaining a New York City apartment and a home in rural upstate New York. Why is this significant? I find it ironic that, although Mary was the closest in geographic proximity to me, she was the cast member who was the toughest to get to meet and consent to an interview for *The Walnut Times*.

A co-worker from Kingston, New York, knew of my newsletter publication and told me he had read in the newspaper that Mary would be doing a book signing at the Merritt Bookstore in Millbrook, New York. He thought I might be interested in attending. He was correct.

I had contacted Mary's administrative assistant and publicist several times and requested an interview for the newsletter. The usual response was that Mary was "not available at this time." But I had pretty much decided that I would keep at it and try to secure that interview. Subscribers kept asking and I was determined to do what I could to include an interview with Mary.

I decided to go down to the book signing, a short trip by car that would take me a little over an hour from my home in upstate New York. My goal was to see if I might be able to introduce myself while passing through the line and express my interest in doing an interview.

As I exited the highway and found my way to the bookstore, I realized that this book signing was going to be "an event." Cars were parked everywhere—in parking lots, along the side of the road—and clusters of people were making their way to the bookstore. The line of people was already out the door. I managed to find a place to park my car and hurried to get a spot in line.

There had to be 200 people ahead of me in a line that wound around the inside of the store, weaving adjacent to the table where Mary was signing her book, up the stairs to a second level, and back down past the table a second time.

Mary had an assistant there to help get the book open to the page where she would sign, and the owner of the bookstore was also willingly taking photos of Mary with fans as she signed each of their books.

An hour passed and it was finally my turn. As she was finishing up with the person ahead of me, I handed my camera to the owner so he could take a photo or two and gave my book to her assistant. I got the nod from the assistant and approached the table.

"Hi, Mary," I said. "It's nice to meet you. My name is David Van Deusen."

"How would you like me to sign your book?" Mary asked.

"To Dave, would be fine," I replied. Having observed how quickly people were being ushered by, I continued to talk to her as she began to sign the book.

"Do you know what *The Walnut Times* is?" I asked. "I am the editor of the newsletter and would love to do an interview with you."

Mary's assistant paused and turned to acknowledge my statement.

"We know what *The Walnut Times* is," he said. "It's *The Dick Van Dyke Show* newsletter."

"That's right," I responded. It was clear that he knew who I was and what the publication was all about. Mary also seemed to know what I was talking about.

She finished signing the book and turned her attention toward me. "You should contact PMK regarding an interview, and we'll see what we can do."

"Thanks very much," I replied, "I'll do that." She handed me my book, and I began to move toward the other side of the table. As I was starting to leave, I noticed that I had also gotten the attention of another man who was sitting near the book signing table reading the newspaper. It was

Mary's husband, Dr. Robert Levine. Dr. Levine looked up and gave me a nod of acknowledgement as I passed by.

From what I could judge by the reaction of my request, I got the sense that an interview might be a realistic possibility. And although it took a few more months of contacts to publicists, coordination, and persistence, the interview finally took place with Mary by telephone. She spoke with me from her office in New York City.

TWT: If you happen to be channel surfing late at night and come across *The Dick Van Dyke Show*, do you pause and watch for awhile?

MTM: You bet I do, at least for a little while. I never just run right past it. And I find now that after all these years that I watch the episodes with very little memory of what's going to happen next. So it's always interesting to me.

TWT: Do you have a personal favorite episode?

MTM: Probably for my own reasons "My Blonde-Haired Brunette" is my favorite. That was the first time Carl ever gave me the opportunity to take some comedy and run with it. He obviously was pleased with what I did because, from that point on, I always had something funny to do in the show.

TWT: Does it seem possible that the show was filmed over thirty-five years ago?

MTM: It's hard to believe. From my point of view, if anything dates the show, it is the realization that we never did it in color. And that just seems impossibly ancient.

TWT: Is there a show that you thought didn't come off well or disliked as you look back?

MTM: No, not a one of them. And certainly from my own personal experience, each one was a treasured week spent together, working with the production people and the prop people, to say nothing of the actors. We were a real family.

TWT: Do you have a favorite production number?

MTM: I think that "You Wonderful You" was my favorite. That was a flashback episode to when Rob was in the army and I was a USO entertainer.

TWT: Did you and Dick get to choreograph your dance numbers?

MTM: No, we didn't. But we probably could have if we had the time. That was always better left to somebody else because we were busy blocking and rehearsing the scenes in the show and wouldn't have had time to do justice to the numbers that we did.

TWT: Did you actually ad lib "Oh Rob," or is that a line that Carl wrote and you just ran with?

MTM: Sometimes it was written, and sometimes it just seemed the appropriate thing to do, and I would ad lib it. But nobody had any idea that it would develop a life of its own. I do lectures from time to time, and, afterwards, during the question and answer period, that expression invariably comes up. Would you do an "Oh Rob" for us? And, of course, I am happy to do that. I usually throw in a "Mr. Grant" just for good measure.

TWT: One of my personal favorite episodes is "The Curious Thing About Women."

MTM: That's certainly my second favorite.

TWT: Do you recall if you ever had the opportunity to rehearse the inflatable boat scene near the end of the show?

MTM: It is my recollection that there was only the one shot, and we had to guess at what the boat was going to do. This was also the first time I was ever given a block of comedy. It was a la the master himself, Dick Van Dyke, and it was terrifying because I saw it there, I spotted it, and I knew that this was the kind of thing that Dick would have a field day with. And I just kept hoping that I would come close to doing justice to the spot, and I guess it did work very well. Another favorite was the episode where we were convinced that there was a mix up in babies, and it turned out that the other father was black. That was a phenomenon for us because, in the editing, they had to shorten the laughs just to keep the audience interested. People at home generally don't laugh as long as they do in the studio. But I tell you that laugh must have gone on for forty-five seconds. It just did not want to stop.

TWT: We have the impression that you are quite a pool player.

MTM: Don't I wish I were. I grew up as a dancer and dancers were always taking dancing classes and never were involved in sports, so my reaction to a ball is so negative and unsportsmanlike when I see one coming at me, my instinct is to duck. And when I try to figure out anything like trajectories in pool or billiards, I am at a complete loss. I guess I can follow directions well enough as long as there is an expert such as we had for that show telling me exactly what to do and when to do it.

TWT: Can you tell us who was the definitive Perquackey champion on *The Dick Van Dyke Show*?

MTM: No question about it, Ann Morgan Guilbert.

TWT: Have you kept in touch with Ann over the years?

MTM: I haven't seen her in a long time. I occasionally see her on screen as *The Nanny*'s grandmother. Let me tell you that that role is real acting because Annie is nowhere near old enough to do that. But she is so delightful, and she was such a good friend, but I live here in New York, and she's in California, so it's hard to keep those friendships going.

TWT: In the "All About Eavesdropping" episode, do you remember if there really was a peanut butter and avocado dip? It's kind of hard to imagine peanut butter and avocado as a dip.

MTM: I agree. It's hard to buy into, isn't it? I don't really remember. So, which brave soul is going to experiment? Somebody must have tried it out. Most likely Carl.

TWT: In the "October Eve" episode when Laura was supposedly painted in the nude, do you recall if there was actually anything at all on the canvas in the art gallery, or was it just a totally blank canvas?

MTM: I don't remember. Maybe Carl or Dick does.

TWT: Do you have any items that you saved from the show?

MTM: I don't have any memorabilia from *The Dick Van Dyke Show*. I guess you don't think about it until it's your show. I do remember a ceramic ashtray from back in the days when people smoked with no guilt, and I had one of those, and it had a caricature of each of us on it. But mine had a crack in it, and it was discarded.

TWT: Have you or Dick ever been approached to reprise your roles as Laura and Rob?

MTM: No, I don't think so.

TWT: Would you ever consider that, or is Laura Petrie a character that you would prefer to be unassociated with after all these years?

MTM: Yes, I think it's a little too far away from that show. You know, I'm doing something like that with the reprise of the Mary Richards and Rhoda characters. I think it's the first time it's ever been done, bringing life back to two characters twenty years later.

TWT: Fans are very excited about the new show.

MTM: I think it stands a very good chance of working as long as we're picking out the good writers, and, so far, I think we are. But with that in mind, I don't see how I could do that and get anybody to believe it, to do it with *The Dick Van Dyke Show*.

TWT: Could you offer some thoughts on the cast members who have left us?

MTM: It stunned me the amount of loss I felt when Morey Amsterdam died, in particular, because he was so integral to the show. Certainly Richard Deacon died first, and that was a sad, sad loss. But the passing of Morey really affected me. I was booked to do the David Letterman show the day that I found out he died, and I had to cancel. Of course, Jerry Paris was our director for *The Dick Van Dyke Show*. It was sad when he passed as well. It was not only Jerry, but he was preceded in death by his wife. I ran into their daughter in an elevator somewhere in Minneapolis or Chicago, and it was just a very quick ride. I told her how much I missed her dad and her mom...then it was her floor, and then it was my floor, and then the ride was over.

TWT: Will you please confirm for us that you are in good health?

MTM: Yes, I am. You know you have to consider the source of those who are saying that I'm about to lose my sight. I do have ongoing vision conditions that have to be dealt with. Thank God that we have the development of the laser and other procedures that keep me sighted. There is no ongoing fear about being blinded. I'm far from that.

TWT: I know I speak for a number of people in applauding you for your diabetes causes and the money that you raise there.

MTM: Thank you. I work very hard for the Juvenile Diabetes Foundation.

TWT: What is the absolute favorite role that you have ever had?

MTM: I'm unable to choose just one. There are three very important career points in my life so far. They are *The Dick Van Dyke Show*, *The Mary Tyler Moore Show*, and *Ordinary People*. And there were some wonderful things in amongst those others that I'm terribly proud of, but those have to stand out as the highlights.

TWT: Is there anyone that you would like to work with that you haven't had the opportunity?

MTM: There are all kinds of wonderful actors out there. I really enjoy working with good actors, and the key to that is listening. I think that's one of the first things that Dick Van Dyke and Carl Reiner communicated to me. The ability to listen and to appreciate humor, and I do that. I try to do that in the dramatic things that I do, too, because in life all people have humor, to one degree or another, with them, and they are better people if they can utilize it and make the most of it.

TWT: Do you have a particular sitcom or two that you enjoy watching today?

MTM: I love *Seinfeld* and *Mad About You* and *Dharma and Greg*. I think that's a very good show. And *Friends*, although the age difference is such that I don't really identify with their situations, but I can certainly appreciate the writing.

TWT: Do you have a most cherished award or honor that you've gotten?

MTM: I am the proud possessor of seven Emmys. I keep them on the bookshelf in my office.

As the interview came to a close, I thanked Mary and let her know that it was very nice to have finally talked with her. She indicated that she enjoyed receiving *The Walnut Times* and would look forward to reading the next issue.

Throughout the years that have passed since our interview, my contact with Mary has been very limited. I asked if she would like to participate in the walnut documentary, and, although she considered it initially, she ultimately declined my request. Too bad! I would like to have had her give her firsthand account of sliding down that huge pile of walnuts! Wouldn't you?

From my perspective as a fan, Mary seems to be much more of a private person and, as such, I have never really gotten to know her like I have gotten to know the other cast members from the show. At the same time, I was appreciative of her willingness to do an interview and participate in my "nutty" endeavor.

# 10

## *Larry Mathews*

It took me a long time to finally convince Larry Mathews to consent to an interview with me for *The Walnut Times*.

As Larry tells it, he had been burned many times by others who had interviewed him regarding his role on *The Dick Van Dyke Show*. The press would often misquote him, print incorrect information, or "twist around" what he had told them during their interviews.

Having previously engaged all of the major cast members except Larry, I was determined to do what I had to do to ensure his participation. I continued to pursue him at every opportunity and let him know that I was still interested in doing an interview. My perseverance ultimately paid off when Larry finally yielded to my request, with one stipulation.

Larry asked for, and I agreed that he could have, full approval of the text of the article. Absolutely! Why not? I could understand and appreciate Larry's frustrations from the previous interviews he had done. At the same time, I certainly had no intentions of misquoting or slanting anything he said, in any way, so I had no issues with Larry reviewing and editing anything that I had written.

I eventually interviewed Larry by telephone from his office in Los Angeles. Before the article made it to *The Walnut Times*, I provided my final version of the interview for his review, and it came back to me without a single edit, having received his full endorsement.

TWT: How old were you when you were cast in the role of Ritchie?
LM: I was five.
TWT: Do you recall your audition?

LM: It was with Carl. He asked me to sit on the couch and do some lines from the pilot episode. And he really liked it. And I never read with Dick or Mary before I got the part. Carl made the decision with Danny and Sheldon. I found out years later that I guess it came down to choosing between me and another boy. Carl wanted to go with somebody that had never really done anything before, and that's how I fell into the right place at the right time.

TWT: Tell us about being a kid on the set of a TV show. Did you have a tutor?

LM: Yes, you had to have a tutor. That was required. So I would go in and do my schooling pretty much in the morning. They would try and save the afternoon for any rehearsals and whatever we were doing. But every so often they would interrupt class and have me come in during the day, and we'd make up the class time later. I actually skipped a grade while I was being tutored.

TWT: At the time that *The Dick Van Dyke Show* was shooting at Desilu Cahuenga, what else was in production there?

LM: *Make Room for Daddy* or *The Danny Thomas Show* was in production. When we first started, *The Joey Bishop Show* was there. *Andy Griffith* was also shooting at the time.

TWT: Did you have a chance to hang out with Ron Howard?

LM: No. The only person I saw regularly was Angela Cartwright, and she was cool. Ron was way down at the end of the lot, and I never really wandered down there that much. Interestingly, though, I knew Ron because we both grew up in Burbank and had played in the same Little League together. I really got to know Joey Bishop very well and would see him quite a bit. Joey taught me how to throw a football. In later years, when *I Spy* had moved onto the lot, Bill Cosby and Robert Culp would come out, and we would throw the football around.

TWT: It's interesting to look back now and see how many of the guest stars who appeared on *The Dick Van Dyke Show* would also end up in roles on the other shows being produced on the lot.

LM: All of the shows that I mentioned were Danny Thomas and Sheldon Leonard shows. They really had that whole lot tied up with their products. All of the production companies were set up independently, but the two main people that were involved in every one of them were Sheldon Leonard and Danny Thomas. In turn, there would be a lot of crossovers between here and there with different shows. Guest stars that they would use on one show would often move on to another.

TWT: As you look back, was there anyone particularly in the cast that you seemed to have a special bond with?

LM: Rose Marie and I have always had a special friendship because we share the same birthday. Jerry Paris and I also had a really nice relationship. Sometimes I would go over and spend the night at his house with his son Tony. But in general, there was a lot of love and good relationships between all of us for different reasons.

TWT: How would you categorize your remembrance of Sheldon?

LM: Sheldon was one of the most wonderful men I've ever met or will ever meet in my life. He was not only a boss, but he was a friend and a father figure and all that rolled into one. You could always go and talk to him, and he would help you in any way he could. He was really just something special. I love him.

TWT: Many child stars seem to encounter so many problems or trouble with the law, drug problems, and more. Yet you didn't experience those types of problems. How do you account for your success?

LM: I attribute most of it to my family and my parents. My mother was with me there on the set the whole time. And when we came home from work, we were just part of the family. There was no special this, no special that. I was just one of the brothers and sisters. My parents also really kept the focus correct and made sure that I knew that this was just a fun thing and a job I was doing.

TWT: Do you have a particular favorite episode?

LM: My favorite episode from a performance standpoint was "Never Name a Duck." There was a scene when Rob had taken the duck away, and I had to cry. And I had never done that before. It is the thing I'm most proud of. I actually went to my mother, and I remember asking her how I should cry for the scene. She sent me to Sheldon for help. He proceeded to tell me a really gut wrenching story how his dog was killed. In about five minutes, I was a mess. But I went on stage and did one of my better serious type performances.

TWT: Any others?

LM: I also liked the woodpecker episode for myself in terms of how I performed. I also enjoy watching "It May Look Like a Walnut" and "The Ghost of A. Chantz," which I wasn't even in, but I think is a great episode.

TWT: So, give us the inside scoop. We enter the front door of the Petrie home and go in your bedroom. What's back there Larry?

LM: There's nothing at all, it's just backstage. That was the way back into the dressing rooms.

TWT: As you approach the bedroom door, there appears to be a hallway behind the brick wall.

LM: You could get to the kitchen from there, but it was just behind the set.

TWT: Do you have any memorabilia from the show?

LM: Believe it or not, I have Alan Brady's desk!

TWT: How did you ever get that?

LM: When I got out of college in the late 1970s, I went to work for Ron Jacobs at *Danny Thomas Productions*. At some point in time, they had all kinds of props stored down at MGM that had to be moved. And they told me if I wanted anything that I could take it. There was this really cool desk that I ended up taking. Several years later I caught an episode of *The Dick Van Dyke Show* where they showed Alan's office and desk, and I suddenly realized that the desk I had in my house was the "Alan Brady" desk!

TWT: Do you still keep in touch with the cast?

LM: Rose Marie and I will send each other Christmas cards and birthday cards every year and say hello. I see Dick often. We got together to do the Chairman's Choice special for Nick at Nite, and that was a lot of fun. We had a good time shooting the segments. And I also attended the dedication of Dick's star on the Hollywood Walk of Fame along with Carl, Sheldon, and Morey.

TWT: When the show ended its five year run, you were eleven. What did you do then?

LM: I went back to school and hung out with my brothers. I did a lot of theatre when I got into high school at Notre Dame High and was also a Theater Arts major at UCLA. When I got out of UCLA, I started working in post production and production. I went back and worked for Ron Jacobs for awhile and then went over to work for Tony Thomas, Danny's son, for a couple of years on *Soap* and *Benson*.

TWT: Are you married?

LM: Yes. My wife's name is Jennifer. We were married on Valentine's Day. We have two German shepherds. I've always had this thing for German Shepherds, and I could never figure it out. One day I started thinking about why I love shepherds so much, and I finally realized why. Remember the episode where Buddy had to leave Larry, the German shepherd, and I went into the cupboard to hide from the dog? Being scared of the dog was a good bit of acting. In actuality, the minute I saw a dog I went up to it, stuck my face in, and started hugging it. He was the most wonderful dog in the world.

TWT: As you look back at *The Dick Van Dyke Show*, what are your sentiments?

LM: *The Dick Van Dyke Show* is an American icon. But at the time, we never knew it would be a classic. We were doing a show and having a good time. To think that forty years later it would still be on the air. It's as pertinent now as it was then. Carl is such a brilliant man. I think I can be so bold to say that this show was something that you'll never really see again in your life. *The Dick Van Dyke Show* was a really wonderful piece of my life that I am very grateful for, and fortunate that I was able to do.

The interview was relaxed and very comfortable. As it progressed, I think it became quickly apparent to Larry that I was a real, diehard fan of *The Dick Van Dyke Show* and he had had nothing to worry about from the standpoint of being misquoted.

The issue of *The Walnut Times* was published soon after and was very well received by subscribers. Fans had waited a long time for Larry's interview, and they were not disappointed. Larry's experiences offered a very unique and extremely interesting perspective—one that only he could offer as the youngest member of *The Dick Van Dyke Show* cast.

During my trip to Los Angeles in September 2002, Larry invited me to stop by and meet him in person at his office. We had a terrific visit!

We discussed the then future plans to release *The Dick Van Dyke Show* on DVD and how great it would be to have full, uncut, pristine versions of the show for our personal archives.

We also had a great time talking about the show and comparing our DVDS memorabilia collections. Larry has many show related photos and scripts as well as some other unique items.

Of particular interest is a copy of the Big Bad Brady poster which was used in the final episode of the series, "The Gunslinger." What is unique about this poster is that Larry's mom encouraged him to go around at the cast party and have the entire cast and crew members sign it for him. Little did Larry realize in 1966 at that final gathering what a treasured item he would have many years later.

I was thrilled to learn that Larry had, among the scripts in his collection, a copy of the "It May Look Like a Walnut" script. Larry graciously offered to provide me with a copy of "Walnut" to supplement the other scripts which I had managed to obtain over the course of several years of collecting. Due to the connection between this specific episode and the newsletter, I think this script is one of my finer collectibles.

It's very cool to see lines "in print" in the script that never made it to the actual cut of the episode. Like what you ask?

Remember Buddy following up to Rob's observation of "You know a funny thing" with the reply "Yeah, I know a funny thing. A nearsighted turtle falling in love with an army helmet."

Buddy's original line was written "Yeah, I know a funny thing. A nearsighted turtle *making love* to an army helmet." Do you think the network censors might have had a role in this change?

How about the scene where Sally explains to Buddy why she could never marry Kolak because of Kolak's four eyes? "Buddy, you know my mother is against interplanetary marriages!"

Then there was the dialogue where Mel tells Rob that Laura was against having Danny Thomas on the show—that she wanted Kolak. Buddy replies, "We all wanted Kolak, but here on Earth he isn't a big enough name." "Yet," says Sally!

Even more intriguing is to note those lines that actually made it into the episode that were *not* included in the final version of Carl's storyline.

Danny Thomas enters the writer's office and Rob is trying to figure out who he really is. Danny's original line in reply to Rob's questioning was written "I've been told that I look like your Danny Thomas." This line was ultimately transformed into the well known and classic utterance "What is a Danny Thomas?" Can't you recall the expression on Danny's face as he says this line?

Believe it or not, the widely remembered and often fan quoted line "I have perfect 20 20 20 20 vision" is *not* in the script. Wouldn't you love to know how this line found its way into the ultimate version of the episode?

Finally, as Danny leaves the office humming a tune and tossing a few stray walnuts over his shoulder, we find Rob trying to make sense of who was just there in the office and what has really just happened.

Talking to himself, Rob's original line read, "That wasn't Kolak. That was Danny Thomas. I recognized his theme song and his nose!"

The next time you watch this episode, envision these "alternate" lines of dialogue for some added viewing pleasure. What fun!

At the time of this writing, Larry continues in the entertainment business as the Vice President of Sales for a full service post production facility serving motion picture, television, and multimedia clients.

During my most recent trip to LA in 2005, Larry and I decided to get together for lunch. I thought to myself. This might finally be it! What is "it" you ask? Keep reading!

Recalling how Ritchie went off to school with his lunch bag full of walnuts, I half hoped that Larry might show up at the restaurant with his own bag of walnuts in hand and dole out a few for me—less the absorbitron, of course.

But it was not to be so during this visit! I guess he's still hoarding the walnuts all for himself! Maybe next time when we get together for lunch!

In all seriousness, through both my admiration, and our genuine, mutual appreciation of *The Dick Van Dyke Show,* Larry and I have become great friends. I expect that we will remain so for many years to come.

# 11

## *Behind the Camera*
## *Sam Denoff, John Rich, Bud Molin, Frank Butler*
## *Writer, Director, Editor, Announcer*

The smell of cigar greeted Fred and me as we walked through the door of Sam Denoff's office. Sam was on the telephone when we arrived and had briefly interrupted his conversation to call to us outside the office door to tell us to let ourselves in.

While he finished his phone call, we wandered around the office and observed the many show business artifacts that decorated his surroundings.

Sam Denoff is the Denoff half of the well-known "Persky and Denoff" duo and was one of the key script writers and eventual producers of *The Dick Van Dyke Show*.

Sam had initially responded to a letter I had written to him asking about his role on the show. I probably should have known better when asking a comedy writer to respond to such open ended questions. You'll see what I mean!

TWT: Please tell us a little about yourself.

SD: I was born in Brooklyn, New York, the second son of Esther and Harry Denoff on July 1, 1928. I was an extraordinarily beautiful child and have remained beautiful my entire life. I graduated from Great Neck High School on Long Island and went to Adelphi College in Garden City, New York.

TWT: How did you break into show business and end up writing for *The Dick Van Dyke Show*?

SD: My first job in show business was as an NBC Page in New York. In 1954, I got a job at radio station WNEW where I met Bill Persky. We worked there for seven years writing jingles, jokes, and material for stand-up comics. Our first job in television was for the new *Steve Allen Show* on ABC. That was in 1961, and that gig got us to California. We then did the *Andy Williams Show* and then wrote free-lance half hour scripts for shows like *McHale's Navy, Joey Bishop*, etc. Our goal was to be able to write for the only show that mattered to us…you guessed it… *The Dick Van Dyke Show*. And, in 1962, we wrote our first script for the show, and well, our lives changed.

TWT: Can you describe your relationship with Bill Persky?

SD: My relationship with Bill Persky, then and now, is quite close. He now lives in New York City. The reason our partnership broke up was because I wanted children and he didn't.

TWT: Can you describe your relationship with Carl Reiner?

SD: Carl Reiner is a great man. He is my friend, my teacher, my professional father. However, he is NOT a good dancer.

TWT: Were you and Persky given the latitude to come up with your own story ideas?

SD: Of course we developed ideas of our own, but they all had to be approved by Carl and my other God, Sheldon Leonard, without whom there would be no *Dick Van Dyke Show*.

TWT: As writers for the show, did you also attend the filming of the episode?

SD: Yes. Once we started writing scripts for the show, we were at every filming. That's how we learned the process.

TWT: Did you join in the weekly cast parties after the filming of a show?

SD: There were never any cast parties. Everyone hated each other and was glad to leave as soon as the director said "It's a wrap." Of course we were included, you nit wit. However, we were not allowed to speak.

TWT: Was there ever a show that was written but never filmed?

SD: I believe there were some scripts that were never shot, but I don't remember what they were about or how many. There were never any episodes shot that were not aired.

TWT: Do you have a particular episode that stands out as a favorite?

SD: I've been asked that question a lot. A few of my favorites are "Coast-to-Coast Big Mouth," "October Eve," and "I'd Rather Be Bald, Than Have No Hair at All." My favorite still has to be the first one we wrote, "That's My Boy." That show that kicked off season three and the beginning of our real career.

TWT: Do you still watch the show today?

SD: When I can, I watch the show, having forgotten a lot of the stuff. And, because of Carl's influence it still works, thirty years later. Not a lot of shows can boast that relevance and longevity.

TWT: Do you still stay in touch with *The Dick Van Dyke Show* family?

SD: I keep in touch with Dick and speak with Mary often. We try to see each other when she is on this coast or I go to New York. I see Carl all the time, and Rosie once in a while.

TWT: What have you done since *The Dick Van Dyke Show*?

SD: What have I done since *The Dick Van Dyke Show*??? Didn't you hear? For the last twenty-seven years I have been in San Quentin serving consecutive terms for repeated acts of exhibitionism and pedophilia and civil rights violations against rodeo clowns. Seriously, I have kept very busy since the show ended in 1966. Bill and I were the Executive Producers of *That Girl*, starring Marlo Thomas, which ran from 1966 to 1970. In 1966 we also created and produced *Good Morning World*. Other series followed, such as: *The Funnyside, Big Eddie, The Montefuscos, Lotsa Luck*, starring Dom Deluise. In 1967, we co-wrote the *Sid Caesar Special* and earned another Emmy. In 1968, we wrote and produced the first *Bill Cosby Special* for which we won still another Emmy. Other acclaimed specials which we wrote and produced were: *The Julie Andrews Special* with Gene Kelly; *The First Nine Months Are The Hardest, Dick Van Dyke and The Other Woman* with Mary Tyler Moore, and *Pure Goldie*. In the mid-seventies, Bill and I broke up. Subsequently, I went on to produce *The Practice* starring Danny Thomas, create and produce *The Don Rickles Show*, produce *On Our Own, Turnabout*, create and produce *The Lucie Arnaz Show* and serve as Executive Supervising Producer of *It's Garry Shandling's Show*.

TWT: How would you describe your overall experience being involved with the show?

SD: Working on *The Dick Van Dyke Show* was the single most rewarding and nurturing and nourishing experience of my professional life…except for the time I was locked in a hotel room for three days with Claudia Schiffer.

Now do you understand what I meant?

Sam finished his phone call and came around from behind his desk and sat down with Fred and me in the living room area of the office.

"Did you see my scripts from the show over there on the shelf?" Sam was pointing to his collection of scripts that he and Persky had written.

"Let me go get the Artanis painting," he said, "so you can see that. I'll also bring down the painting that Carl and Dick did with water pistols at the end of the 'October Eve' episode. Each of those was nearly tossed in the trash dumpster, but I managed to grab them before they were lost."

Sam went upstairs and returned in a few minutes with not two, but three paintings. It seems that there were two versions of the Artanis painting done by Art Director, Ken Reid, and Sam had salvaged them both before they ended up in the garbage. One was used early in the show, and one was used near the end of the episode.

Two versions of the famous Artanis painting

After we finished looking at those two paintings, Sam showed us the famous squirt gun painting. The painting still displayed the signatures of Carl Reiner and Dick Van Dyke. Very cool! As we wrapped up our visit, Sam got right into the action and took a great picture with me. And although you'll see from the picture that he still has his thumbs, I am pretty sure he has lost his sense of humor! We had a great time with Sam!

Sam and I are frequently in contact with each other by email just to drop a line and say hello. Sam has been a great help to me in facilitating contact with other members of the cast and crew and also contributed to various issues of the newsletter. And I'm hoping that one day he can also introduce me to Claudia Schiffer!

I had written several letters to John Rich asking if he would consider being interviewed for *The Walnut Times*. I was disappointed that I never received a reply.

I recalled the discussions that I had with Rose Marie when she described the wonderful friendship that John and she had maintained over the years. I wondered if she might help to facilitate an interview for me with John.

The next time I wrote to Rose Marie, I asked if she might put in a good word for me with John. She did one better. She gave John a call and told him all about me and the newsletter. She wrote me back with John's phone number and told me that he was expecting my call.

When I phoned John, he was very cordial and happy to talk with me about *The Dick Van Dyke Show* and other aspects of his career. He did make a point of telling me that he did not routinely do interviews. However, he indicated that he was doing this interview with me because of all the good things that Rose Marie had to say about me. Many thanks to Rose Marie!

TWT: Please tell us a little bit about your background. When did you first start directing? Did you go to film school?

JR: No. I had been a sports broadcaster at the University of Michigan while I was in my graduate year. I was the announcer for Michigan basketball. That's how I started in show business. Then I went to New York and couldn't get a job. I hooked up with a former Michigan student, and together we came up with a show called *Wanted* which was the first of the shows whose premise was chasing "wanted" people. That was NBC Radio in 1950. And that's really how I got into television. They wanted me to do it on TV, and I said no way. I told them that I wanted to be a director in this new medium. And everybody in radio laughed at me. I told them, kiddingly, that they would all be working for me in two years, and that's exactly what happened. I had to get in on the ground floor of the television explosion. So I started very young, barely out of college.

TWT: Did you know any of *The Dick Van Dyke Show* cast members prior to your arrival on the set?

JR: Yes. I knew Rose Marie. I had cast her previously in a role on an episode of *Gunsmoke*.

TWT: Can you tell us some more about that?

JR: I knew of Rose Marie, of course, because she was a well-known performer. She came in to the audition as a comedienne, but the role that she was supposed to play was that of a country woman chopping wood. She really thought she was in the wrong room because she couldn't believe she would be considered for such a part. But I just asked her to read. I was looking for someone that had a comic turn and knew how to deliver a line. You talk about somebody who can do no wrong. Rose Marie read it perfectly. I told her that I liked her very much, but I asked if she would cut her nails if she got the part. She agreed. I guess people are not used to directors making observations like that. She was stunned that I would pick up on the "well-manicured" nails.

TWT: Do you remember anything else about her appearance?

JR: During the filming, we were doing a scene where she had to serve some food. She was doing it as we would say "full out." I took her aside and said, "Rosie, if you do what you're doing, you'll steal the scene. For God's sake, cut it out." She said, "What am I doing?" She was playing the sketch "full out," and she didn't even realize it. It was great, but it was just over the top for that moment. We have been lifelong friends ever since. I was so pleased when I got her on the show. She is just wonderful.

TWT: How was it that you came to be involved with *The Dick Van Dyke Show*?

JR: Sheldon Leonard and I were both on the Board of Directors of the Director's Guild, and I was in my Western period at that time. I was directing things like *Gunsmoke, Bonanza, Bat Masterson, The Plainsman, The Rifleman*, all of those shows. One day at a board meeting, Sheldon asked, "Did you ever think of coming back out of the muck and mire and doing an indoor show? I've got this thing called *The Dick Van Dyke Show*." So he set up a meeting at Carl Reiner's home. That was when I first met Dick. I told him that I really enjoyed him in a local musical play called *Vintage 60s*. Dick did one of those wonderful things he used to do.

He put his fingers on his nose and said, "No, that was Dick Patterson." Whoops! So that was my first gaffe. But we got along fine.

TWT: Do you recall your first meeting with the cast?

JR: Yes, I do. Let me tell you a story. I had a lot of my experience working in the field of single cameras. In those situations, you would rehearse a scene that was a little bit more than two or three minutes in length. Then you would commit it to film. But you would rehearse it and then get it polished up and then shoot it. That was the technique. On my first day with the *Van Dyke* group, the company was really hot. I could tell right away this was a good group. So I started to get them whipped up into shape. And before you knew it, I had finished the entire rehearsal in the first day, which was Wednesday. Now we didn't shoot until the following Tuesday. And they were hot! Everybody was excited. They liked me. I liked them. And we were getting comic moments, and it was terrific. Suddenly, I realized I had made an awful mistake. I was like the coach that gets the football team up for Sunday's game when it's only Monday. So now I had a completely well-rehearsed episode on Wednesday but nearly a week still left until we filmed. I came in the next day, and they were all excited and I said, "Let's do that again. That was great fun." Then I said, "You know, I've had some second thoughts about that." And they said, "What?" I said, "I'm not sure I like the way the room is configured. Indulge me a little bit. Let's move the couch over here and put the table over there." And I ripped up the set. Turned it around completely. And they were looking at me like I was daft. And they said, "Why are you doing this? It was such a wonderful experience yesterday." I said "Yeah, I know that was good, but, if we were that good yesterday, we've got the time to see if we can improve it. Let's see if this works better." It was all a ruse, of course. I just deliberately wasted the whole day. And the cast was looking at me with daggers and saying, "How could you do this? What's going on?" And I said, "Nothing. I'm just experimenting." We'll be all right." Now it was Friday, and they were a little disgruntled when they came in. And I said, "You know what? I think maybe you guys were right, and the way the set was organized on Wednesday is the way we should do it." So I put it back, and there was a great sigh of relief. Then they caught themselves up, but they weren't completely finished. They had a little way to go because Monday was camera day. But I was able to bring them along the way you would bring a team along. And I told them later what had happened. I realized that I had gotten them ready way too soon.

TWT: Can you explain how the show was filmed and describe your role as director?

JR: The show was filmed before a live audience with three cameras, each shooting a reel of film. A single audio track accompanied the reels of film.

TWT: How did editing take place?

JR: On the Wednesday morning after we had filmed on Tuesday night, the cast would have a reading of the next week's script while the cutting crew would be assembling the film. Wednesday was generally a shorter day when we would read around the table and do very little staging. When we broke for the day, I would go to the cutting room to start the editing process. I would take a little bit of this and a little bit of that and put it on a fourth reel. That reel becomes the composite reel.

TWT: As the director, did you call all of the camera shots?

JR: Absolutely. Every single move is planned.

TWT: Do you have a particular favorite *Dick Van Dyke Show* episode?

JR: My favorite is also Dick's favorite, the "Where Did I Come From?" episode. I did a few tricks in that one. Watch the segment where the alarm clock rings, and Dick jumps out of bed and heads for the dresser where Laura's suitcase is. In that scene, Dick lifted the handle of the suitcase and then went on and did the next piece of acting. When I looked at the film, I wished he had done that maneuver twice because it was just too quick. Then I thought to myself, wait a minute, I'm on film here. So I reprinted the piece of film, and, for all practical purposes, I had him do it twice. Look at that show if you can. You'll see Dick raises the lid to make sure that he's got it in the right position, and then we cut to Mary whose giving him a look of disgust. Then I had him do that thing twice by repeating the piece of film. And it made the joke work. The other episode that I really like is when Dick makes a mistake about the black child ("That's My Boy!"). That's my second favorite.

TWT: Do you have any other special remembrances?

JR: Dick's ability to handle props is legendary. He is the best prop actor I have ever worked with, bar none. We had a sequence where Morey and Rosie are in the writers' room and Dick comes tap dancing in and twirling down stage, and they look at him in surprise at the happy entrance. Dick takes his hat off and, with great theatrical gesture, flings it towards the hat rack (which is up by the door). In rehearsal, we discussed how great it would be if he could stick the hat on the rack, realizing, of course, that it was nearly impossible. He tried several times without success. In the end, Carl decided that it didn't matter if Dick landed the hat—it was his attitude that mattered. So we rehearsed all week long, and Dick kept trying, but he never once made it. But the gesture was always there, and the hat would fly in the direction of the hat rack and fall. So now we move forward to the night of the filming. Dick comes dancing down stage, twirls, throws the hat, and it sticks on the peg! Without missing a beat, Morey jumps up and shouts, "Did you see that? He's been trying to do this all week and he never could do it." I must have stood there for five or six seconds, open-mouthed, furious. I finally croaked out "cut." I approached Morey, uttered an expletive, and asked, "How could you do that?" Morey mumbled back, "I ruined the take, didn't I?" "Yes, you ruined the take," I said, "you've got to stay in character." Morey was contrite, and I was ticked off. I gave instructions to go back and pick up the scene from where Morey was talking to Rosie just prior to Dick's entrance. At this point, I'm really depressed. We start the cameras, and they do the scene. Here comes Dick in with a glowing attitude, and he tap dances downstage, turns around, flings the hat, and it sticks on the pole. Unbelievable! And the audience went berserk. Of course, in a funny way, it was almost too much because now they were in on the fact that it had failed. But we got it. You look back at that episode and see what you think. That's one of my favorite stories, how the actors can screw you up, even nice actors.

TWT: Any other stories that would interest fans of the show?

JR: I don't know if fans were ever aware of it, but I had a particular conceit with regard to the episodes I directed. When I went into the prop department on the first day, I noticed that there was a dartboard hanging on the wall. I told the prop guy to take the dartboard and hang it in the office. Then I told him to take the twelve darts and put them into the wall—all of them having missed the dart board—as if the writers had put this up on the first day, tried the game and missed, and then never touched it after that. Nobody ever made any comment about it, but, if anybody was sharp enough, they would see that there was not one single dart in the board. They were all in the wall. This brings us to another prop story from the "Hustling the Hustler" episode. If you recall the episode, Morey was starting to clean up the office. They had had a day's work, and there were papers all over the place, and the trick was we had to get Morey out of the office so that his brother (played by actor Phil Leeds) could arrive at the office and start the dialogue with Dick. What was actually written was Dick said, "Go ahead Buddy, I'll clean up the office." That was to get Buddy out. Well, cleaning up the papers went as far as it could, but it was over in less than ten seconds. I was a stickler for as close to realistic as possible, so I realized that we needed more time for Morey to get away before Blackie could get into the same elevator and arrive at the office. What could we do to kill some time? I told Dick to pick up the papers to start us off. Then I told him to go over to the wall and take out the twelve darts. I asked if he thought he could take all twelve darts in one hand and fling them all at once and, of course, in an ideal world, stick them in the wall and not hit the board at all. Dick just gave me a look. Do you know that he did the impossible again? Take a look at the show, and you will see he goes across the room, puts a fist full of darts in his hand, and flings them toward the board all at once. And I couldn't get it all in one cut. I had to cut because it was too far away, too wide. But it was an honest cut. We did not fake it. Dick was magnificent. As for the dartboard, that was my little gag. And it was up all the time that I was directing.

TWT: Do you have any keepsakes or memorabilia from the show? Did you keep any scripts of the episodes that you directed?

JR: Mostly scripts. I have one slate, the camera C slate that has my name on it with a powder puff that they used to erase the chalk when they were writing the theme up. Dick also gave me a cigar humidor for a Christmas gift in 1961.

TWT: Do you have any regrets about your work on the show?

JR: My biggest regret is that I didn't get to do the walnut show although I had read the script, and that one would have been the next one up for me. It was a real winner. That was the one that got away. Actually, it was one of several that got away that I wish I could have done, but you can't be everywhere. I had to move on and do my film.

TWT: As you look back at your work from those days, what is your sentiment?

JR: I'm very proud of our work and very lucky to have been there. The strange thing about our work on those shows was that we never thought we were doing a classic. We were going to work and making a living. And maybe that's why it's so good, because we were dedicated. We tried to do something funny and instructive. And who would think that so many years later that the shows would still be as popular as they are today?

John and I have stayed in touch over the years. We have yet to meet in person although we hope to do so one day when I'm in LA and our schedules permit. John continues to be an ardent supporter of the publication, and I am very appreciative of his support of the newsletter.

If you watch the closing credits of *The Dick Van Dyke Show*, the name Bud Molin is one you are sure to recognize. Bud offered some unique insights into this technical aspect of the show when I interviewed him for the newsletter.

TWT: Tell us about the role as film editor on the show. Was it part of your job that you were there during the actual filming of the show?

BM: Yes, I was there. We had a three camera set up. Each camera was loaded with film, and they all ran constantly. John Rich or Jerry Paris (the directors) would stage the show and determine at the same time what each camera was going to capture during the show's performance. The center camera was always like your master. No matter what happened, you could always go to that shot. They would figure out floor moves, where each camera would move to during the show. There was also a camera coordinator up in the booth connected to each camera by radio, and he would call cues as to where each of the cameras should move.

TWT: This explains how the video portion was captured on film. How was the audio recorded?

BM: There was a set of microphones to pick up the audience that was over the audience's head, and then there was a boom shot that would follow the dialogue like you would do in any other movie. There was an audio technician set up in the booth, and he would control where each track would go. If there was going to be a laugh and he knew that, he would open that pot so that you got the laughter recorded. In general, there was a huge technical set up in the booth, and I would be up there with the director assuring him that although a particular shot was missed that I had another shot that I could use.

TWT: Could you see what the cameras were shooting at the time on some kind of a monitor?

BM: No, you couldn't see anything. But you just knew from experience because of where the cameras were located.

TWT: How did the show get edited after it was filmed? Did the director sit down with you to do the editing?

BM: I would do the original edit all by myself and then run it for him for his comments. He would ask for revisions, and we'd make whatever changes he thought was best.

TWT: How did you technically accomplish this editing? Did you literally take the three reels of film and splice them together?

BM: You run each reel of film on what we called the "three headed monster." You look at each camera for the entire show and decide if the scene plays better on camera 1 or camera 2 or camera 3. As you did this, you would mark on your overall track of the show what camera you wanted to go to at different points in the show. Then my assistant would do a full run through and have all three reels of film running at the same time with what was called a sync machine (synchronization with each other and the track), and he would cut between the shots that had been previously determined.

TWT: And you're keeping track of the length of time that you are running for episode length and commercials?

BM: Oh yes. We always had to get it down to the exact air time. And you were always long. Then you would run the show with the director, the producer, and, usually, Sheldon Leonard and decide what we could do without and what we needed to keep.

TWT: This is before the show would go to Earle Hagen for music?

BM: Yes, Earle never got the show before it was edited down to the right length. You didn't want him to write music that you weren't ultimately going to use. Incidentally, that's the best part financially of the whole operation—the composer—he gets paid every time the show is run.

TWT: Was there any kind of wrap party after the filming of a show?

BM: There wasn't really a party. After the shooting, several of us (Dick, Mary, Carl, the director, my wife and myself, Dick's wife) would go out for supper and a few drinks and chat.

TWT: Do you have any unique stories that come to mind about your involvement with the show? As you know, my publication is based upon the famous walnut episode. Anything in particular about that episode that comes to your mind as you think back in the editing and the walnuts?

BM: I know that it was quite a chore for them to get all the walnuts in there. And they made a deal that everything that wasn't crushed during the show's filming could go back to the company that provided the nuts!

TWT: Due to the elaborate nature of the scene with the walnuts coming out of the closet, was there any pressure to capture it on film in one take?

BM: No. That wasn't a problem. It was a very wide shot when Dick opened the closet door and the eight billion walnuts came out. We kidded around about how we might sell the walnuts ourselves—you know, saying that these were the walnuts that Mary Tyler Moore sat on.

TWT: How has technology changed over time with regard to film editing?

BM: It didn't change that much until about fifteen years ago. They came out with laser editing which was kind of replacing tape, and it was less cumbersome. Now all of the editing is either done on computer or on CDs.

TWT: Were you the guy who was responsible for the compiled blooper reels shown at the end of a season wrap party?

BM: My assistant and I did that. I'll tell you an interesting story about when I was cutting the *I Love Lucy* show. All those years, Desi Arnaz never once ever blew a line or missed a shot, so there was never any blooper footage with him. And he never rehearsed fully with everybody because he was taking care of business. He used to go down, and he would look at a run through and know where he was supposed to be and know his lines. In all those years, he never once fluffed. It was amazing that he could go that long and never screw up.

TWT: Of all the projects you worked on over the course of your career, do you have a favorite show or movie?

BM: My favorite is the movie that I did with Carl and Steve Martin called *Dead Men Don't Wear Plaid*. It was fun because I was able to be very creative with it. There was also a tremendous amount of technical obstacles to overcome.

TWT: As you watch a show like *The Dick Van Dyke Show* that you edited, does it bother you because of what they chop out for syndication?

BM: No. Actually, the shows were really kind of set up with tags on them that you could lose and never lose any information. Towards the end of the show, we came up with a tag you could lose, and we would put in a public service announcement. When the show went into syndication, they could drop those off, and you still wouldn't hurt the show.

TWT: I have read that sometimes, instead of cutting out scenes, the actual speed of the show is increased just enough that it would not be noticeable to the viewer but would get them in under the time constraints of being able to run and still fit commercials in.

BM: That's very common. Actually it's a good thing because you don't hurt anything from the show and still maintain the information you want to give to the viewer.

TWT: Do you have any particular memories of the *Van Dyke Show*—a particular episode or event? Friendships with cast members?

BM: Jerry Paris and I were very, very friendly. Very close. And by a fluke we got together on the show, but, in sitting around talking to each other, we found out that he and I were in the same Kindergarten class at the same time. Jerry had a really good comedy instinct. Jerry and I also worked together on some feature films. Sadly, Jerry died before we had finished the editing on the *Police Academy* film.

TWT: Why do you think *The Dick Van Dyke Show* holds up so well today?

BM: The main reason is that Carl is a very, very honest person, and the shows reflect that honesty. Much of what appeared in the show was based on part of things that happened to him. There are no phony laughs, and there really isn't anything in the shows that couldn't actually happen.

I was ecstatic to meet Bud and his wife Nita in the California desert in January, 2005.

We munched on appetizers and sipped drinks at a local restaurant while both Bud and Nita recounted times gone by of experiences with Dick, Carl, Rose Marie, Larry Mathews, Jerry Paris, and many others. The stories were just fascinating. Bud also told me of his long-tenured friendship with Carl Reiner—a friendship that means a great deal to him.

Our conversations continued at their home and also included Bud pulling out his Dick Van Dyke cuff links as well as a *Dick Van Dyke Show* silver pitcher engraved with each cast member's signatures. I thought I knew about all of the show's memorabilia, but Bud surprised me—much to my delight!

Although we had just met in person for the very first time, Bud and his wife and I established an immediate bond—almost as if we had known each other for years. The Molins are terrific people, and we became and remain fast friends!

The music starts, *The Dick Van Dyke Show* logo flashes on the screen, and the next thing you hear is the very recognizable voice of *Dick Van Dyke Show* announcer, Frank Butler.

TWT: Do you recall how you ended up getting the job to do the voiceover for the opening of *The Dick Van Dyke Show*?

FB: I received a call from my agent to report to Glen Glenn Studios for an audition for possibly being picked for *The Dick Van Dyke Show*. In the end, I was chosen, and I was the announcer for the five years of shows.

Film editor, Bud Molin, trying to keep his thumbs and his sense of humor

TWT: Can you describe for us how you did the reading?

FB: *The Dick Van Dyke Show* was a simple opening—*The Dick Van Dyke Show*, with Dick Van Dyke, Rose Marie, Morey Amsterdam and Mary Tyler Moore. But I did more than just the opening announcing of the cast. I also did all of the promotion spots. "*The Dick Van Dyke Show* is brought to you by"—and then your first commercial came in there. The only thing that was crucial about it, aside from the reading, was the timing. I only had eight and a half seconds for that opening. It was very short. But the overall effect was eight and a half second pieces of material which were used. The sponsor was Proctor & Gamble and was constantly changing products, which meant that I was constantly recording new material.

TWT: Were you watching film footage at the time?

FB: I did what's called a "wild spot," without watching the film.

TWT: As the announcer for the show, did you ever meet the cast?

FB: Sure. I went down to Desilu Studios and watched the taping of one of the first shows. I met them casually and, over time, got to know them all pretty well. Carl was the person who I knew best.

TWT: What other work were you involved with when you got the call to audition for *The Dick Van Dyke Show*? Would we recognize your voice on any other television shows?

FB: I did many shows over the course of my career. I did *Petticoat Junction*, *The Rifleman*, *Banacek*, *The Wild, Wild West*, *Name of the Game*, *Perry Mason*, *Sea Hunt*, *The Real McCoys*, and *The Wonderful World of Disney*.

TWT: What was your reaction when you got the call to ask if you would do the voiceover work for *The Dick Van Dyke Show Revisited*?

FB: It was exciting. I met Carl at CBS in Studio City and we sat around like a couple of kids and shot the breeze for a half hour while they got the studio ready. Then I walked in the studio in front of that microphone just like I'd never left it. I was finished with my work in about forty-five minutes.

TWT: That had to just be a flashback to forty years ago, wasn't it?

FB: Yes, it was. I loved *The Dick Van Dyke Show*, and it was wonderful to visit with Carl and see the old clips again.

TWT: I think the most ironic thing is that it took forty years for you to get an announcing credit because, to the best of my knowledge, you never got a credit on the original show, did you?

FB: You are correct. I never got a credit on the original show. But on the *Revisited* special, this time they gave me a "big" credit, right near the top!

As I was updating the content of *The Walnut Times* website one day, I imagined how entertaining and amusing it would be if I could get "the voice" of *The Dick Van Dyke Show* to "announce" *The Walnut Times* as the web page painted on the screen.

I gave Frank a call to see if he might consider such a request. Before I could get the question out of my mouth, Frank had agreed to do the voiceover for me! He was as excited about doing it as I was. Wow! Frank actually did several takes for me, each with its own subtle variation, so I had many choices from which to select. Frank's exclusive audio promotion is just fantastic and serves to give the newsletter a truly genuine association and hook to *The Dick Van Dyke Show*. Stop by the website and have a listen for yourself. It is very cool!

Sam, John, Bud, and Frank have each made his own special contribution toward the success of *The Dick Van Dyke Show*. It has been a sincere pleasure for me to have had the opportunity to get to know these men on a personal level! Thanks guys!

# 12

# *Julie Paris, Bill Idelson, Frank Adamo and the other Guest Stars*

I decided early on in the initial design of the newsletter that I would include a column called the "Guest Star Spotlight" to highlight and acknowledge the contributions of those many performers who made a special or guest appearance on the show.

One of the extremely dominating forces of *The Dick Van Dyke Show* was Jerry Paris—not only for his frequent guest role as Jerry Helper but, probably more importantly, for what he brought to the show as a director. Sadly, Jerry had passed long before I started the newsletter, and I never had the opportunity to interview him.

I did, however, have the fortunate chance to meet up with Julie Paris, Jerry's daughter, at her home in the Los Angeles suburbs, during my first trip west. Julie is an actress herself, having performed in *Pretty Woman, Princess Diaries, Raising Helen*, and, most recently *Princess Diaries II*.

Our association came to be due to the kindness of Ann Guilbert, who was nice enough to forward a letter on to Julie for me to help facilitate our meeting. Julie was very gracious in responding to my request, asking if she would be interested in talking with me about her dad.

We arrived in the early afternoon, and Julie greeted Jack and me at the front door of her home with a big welcome hug. We had talked on the phone only a couple of times, but it was as if we had been friends for a long time. It turns out that this initial meeting was the beginning of a terrific friendship which still endures today.

Since her dad's passing in 1986, Julie has been the keeper of her dad's memorabilia—photos, Emmy award, scripts, his director's chair, and more. During our visit, she unselfishly opened her home to us and allowed us to peruse these tremendous show business-related materials. It was quite a treat. One of the more interesting items was a framed drawing of *The Wizard of Oz* cast which had been done by Dick Van Dyke many years before.

Dick Van Dyke's drawing of *The Wizard of Oz*

As she recalled fond memories, Julie described her dad to us as one of the more friendly guys in all the world.

"If my dad were here," she remarked, "he'd be throwing a big party to welcome you. Our family used to meet people down at the beach, and the next thing we'd know we'd be back at our house having a barbeque with these new friends that we just met! That's just the kind of guy that my dad was!"

Julie told of her frequent visits to the set of *The Dick Van Dyke Show* and recalled how her brother, Tony, and other children of the cast members got the chance to play roles in Ritchie's birthday party episode.

Jerry Paris claimed that the "It May Look Like a Walnut" episode was the first episode that he directed. And although a careful review of the records from that time may indicate otherwise, Carl Reiner believes that Jerry was especially proud of how this particular episode turned out and was quick to declare it as his "first."

"There was some initial hesitancy from the cast when they found out that Jerry was going to direct," explains Carl. "But as soon as they discovered what a talented director Jerry was, they didn't want anyone else. They wanted Jerry!"

As Julie told us more *Dick Van Dyke Show*-related stories, I asked her if she knew what ever became of Bill Idelson, the guy who played Herman Glimsher, Sally's boyfriend. A funny look came over her face.

"What became of Billy Idelson?" she asked. "Why do you want to know? Do you want to meet him?"

Now I was puzzled. Did I want to meet him? Actually, I just wanted to interview him. But all of my previous attempts to contact him for an interview had been unsuccessful. So why was she asking me if I wanted to meet him?

"He lives right down the street," she continued. "Let me give him a call and see if we can stop down."

I couldn't believe my ears. Bill lived just down the street? How lucky could I be to have the chance to meet him, too?

It turns out that the Paris and Idelson families were "real life" next door neighbors and had been very close friends for many years. All of the children had grown up together and remained in close contact for all these years.

Julie made a quick phone call, and, a few minutes later, we were down the street, sitting in Bill Idelson's living room with Bill, his wife, Seemah, and their son, Paul! Julie and Seemah went to the kitchen to chat while Jack and I sat down with Bill and Paul to talk *Van Dyke* and other classic television.

## Julie Paris, Bill Idelson, Frank Adamo and the other Guest Stars

Photo courtesy of Julie Paris

Bill quickly began the conversation by pointing out that, while he is probably best known as Sally's boyfriend, he also played the "you painted it on" bell boy in "Never Bathe on Saturday." I commented that the

"Never Bathe" episode was one of my very favorites, and I thought that his role was one of his very best—just hysterical!

"Did you know that I'm a veteran of old time radio?" Bill asked. "I played the role of 'Rush' in the classic *Vic and Sade* radio program. It was during those early radio days that I met Morey Amsterdam."

As Bill tells it, Morey would stand waiting in the hall outside the radio studio while the live show was going on inside. When the players needed a joke, they would exit the studio to the hallway and tell Morey the subject on which they needed a joke. Morey would come up with the joke, the cast member would pay Morey $5 for the joke and then hurry back into the studio to tell the joke on the air. And Bill witnessed it all. I guess Morey really was the "human joke machine!"

*The Dick Van Dyke Show* was Bill's first comedy show, and he appeared in several episodes as Herman Glimsher. But Bill's contribution to *The Dick Van Dyke Show* as well as many other television shows was usually as a writer/producer. He contributed on three *Dick Van Dyke Show* scripts: "The Square Triangle," "How to Spank a Star," and "Uncle George."

"I have to tell you," laughs Bill, "that, although I got credit on one of those scripts, I think that by the time the final editing was done, that about only one line of my writing ended up in the final version of the episode!" Bill's favorite *Dick Van Dyke Show* episode? "Uncle George!"

Bill is a two-time Writer's Guild Award winner for his work on *The Odd Couple* and *The Bob Newhart Show*. And if you take a look at the credits of many classic TV shows, you're bound to see Bill's name scroll by. In addition to the above, his television credits include *The Twilight Zone, The Andy Griffith Show, Gomer Pyle, Get Smart, Love, American Style, Beans of Boston, Anna and the King,* and *M*A*S*H*.

Bill continued to tell us about a technique he uses to help come up with story concepts.

"I am a big proponent of using a tape recorder to capture ideas and record brainstorming sessions. I think that many good ideas are often lost simply because no one ever gets them down on paper, and then they are forgotten."

I asked for Bill's opinion about the current offerings on television and the originality of the work. Bill's frankness was intriguing.

"Originality doesn't mean shit!" explained Bill. "The audience wants a story that makes their juices flow. They don't care if it's original. The audience is like a little kid who wants to hear the story of *Jack and the Beanstalk* every day. He likes the part where the Giant says 'Fee Fi Fo Fum.' He doesn't give a shit if it's an original story. As a matter of fact, he likes the same story over and over again."

"I told you that Jerry Paris and I were real life neighbors. Let me tell you a funny story about a joke we played on Jerry."

I listened closely as Bill began to tell his story in a very straight, serious tone.

"Jerry was having a very big, fancy party right down the street, and, although we were close friends, we were not invited."

"'What the hell?' I thought. 'He's got a lot of nerve not inviting us. I'll fix him!'"

Bill continued with the story. "So I dressed my four kids in disheveled rags and sent them up to stand outside of Jerry's driveway and beg for money from the arriving guests. It didn't take long for one of the guests to go inside and ask Jerry what was up with the beggars down at the end of his driveway. The kids were just great!"

"Jerry came storming out of the house like a tyrant, ranting and raving at all of the kids, asking them what they were doing. I was standing off to the side out of sight but couldn't contain myself and finally came out into Jerry's view. All of a sudden, he recognized me—and the kids—and realized that he had been the victim of a marvelous practical joke—that I had gotten him good. We had a huge laugh about it!"

Bill penned a book in 1989 entitled *Writing for Dough*. While providing some very frank advice about pursuing a career as a writer, the book is also extremely funny and very entertaining. Pick up a copy, have a read, and see for yourself!

Although semi-retired at eighty-something years of age, Bill continues to write from time to time and still enjoys teaching writing workshops for aspiring writers out of his home. His hobbies include fishing and painting, and much of his artwork is proudly displayed in his home.

As our visit concluded, I wondered if this "chance meeting" was somehow always meant to be. Who would have thought that my off-handed comment to Julie Paris would land us down the street at the home of Bill "Herman Glimsher" Idelson? Bill and his family were so very friendly and just wonderful to us simply due to our mutual appreciation for *The Dick Van Dyke Show*. It was a treat to hear about the life experiences of Bill Idelson.

On my most recent excursion to LA, I was the dinner guest of the Idelsons at their home in the Los Angeles suburbs.

As mutual friend Ann Guilbert once said to me, "The Idelsons are VERY cool people." Ann was absolutely on target with that sentiment. I enjoyed a wonderful evening of home-cooked food and engaging conversation with these "very cool" people who I now call "very cool friends."

## Julie Paris, Bill Idelson, Frank Adamo and the other Guest Stars

*Dick Van Dyke Show* fans recognize the name of Frank Adamo not only as Dick Van Dyke's personal assistant but also as the guy who has credit for the most "bit part" appearances on the show.

Frank was more than willing to share his extensive experiences and memories of working on *The Dick Van Dyke Show*.

TWT: Please tell us about the personal side of Frank Adamo.

FA: I was born in January, 1930, in Long Island, and graduated from public school there. After high school, I first attended a vocational arts school in Manhattan and then went on to Columbia to study set design. When I graduated, the unions weren't really hiring anybody, so I ended up taking a job with the J. Walter Thompson advertising agency. And that's where I met Dick. He used to come in and do Rinso soap commercials. He was also substituting for Gary Moore on daytime television. Through that association, we got to be pretty good friends. Unfortunately, the union cracked down and said I couldn't continue to work at the agency unless I joined the union. J. Walter Thompson would not pay the required fee, so I left there around 1954 or 1955. I started to study dance, which was kind of late because I was now twenty-five, but I was determined that I was going to do something. About this time, I also read in the trade papers that Dick was in rehearsal at the Phyllis Anderson Theater for a musical called *Bye Bye Birdie*. So I went to the theater and waited by the stage door. When Dick came out, he recognized me and asked what I was doing. I told him that I needed work. Dick said he was going to Philadelphia to do the show and that I should meet him there. After reading the trade papers to see when they were going to be there, I got on a bus and headed for Philadelphia. All the time I kept asking myself, what am I going to do when I get there? In the interim, I had found out that Dick did not have a wardrobe person. I discovered that you needed to join the union to be a wardrobe person. And to join the union, you had to pass a sewing exam. It didn't really make much sense to me because I figured if an actor comes off stage and his fly is wide open, you're not going to do anything except put a safety pin on it! Anyway, I passed the test and paid the dues.

TWT: What was Dick's reaction when you arrived on the scene?

FA: He looked very surprised, but I said, "You told me to come!" And Dick said, "Okay, you're here." And that was it. The musical ended up going into New York and, of course, was quite successful.

TWT: How long was it before Dick was offered his TV show?

FA: About a year later, Sheldon Leonard stopped by after a performance and told Dick he was interested in doing a TV pilot. Dick said he would do it and asked if I would come along to California with him. Dick had no idea what he could pay me, but I told him that we would manage. So off he went with his family, and off I went on my own.

TWT: How did you end up being a bit player on the show?

FA: My primary job was to handle administrative items for Dick…setting up appointments, screening calls, answering fan mail, etc. One day Sheldon suggested that I work as a stand in for Dick since he and I were both about the same build. I said fine. I was also present during script readings around the conference table, and, going through a script, they would say, "Let Frank read for the actor that's not here." In the end, Sheldon decided to let me perform the parts.

TWT: Did you get paid two salaries?

FA: Yes, I got what Dick paid me to be his assistant as well as the Union salary. If I uttered one sentence as an extra, I got paid. I also was paid for just being in the background. I think I had the most parts as a non-contract player.

TWT: What was your favorite bit part?

FA: My favorite role was as H. Fieldstone Thorley in the "Henry Walden" episode. I also liked the one where I did a singing telegram. I really stopped the show because I have a terrible voice.

TWT: Can you tell us about your role as the Veterinarian's assistant in "Never Name a Duck"?

FA: I was the assistant who was supposed to handle a kangaroo. So during the day, I went to the trainer to try to get friendly with this beast. I fed him and walked with him a little bit, so he got used to me. Jerry Hausner, who was the actor who I was supposed to hand over the kangaroo to, didn't want to have anything to do with him. Just before I made my entrance, I got stuck in this little cubicle, and when I went out on my cue to hand off the kangaroo, the audience became hysterical. Jerry grabbed the chain, and the kangaroo wasted no time in going right across the stage, dragging Jerry behind him. We had to do several takes to get it. Poor Jerry Hausner, I think he wet his pants!

TWT: Do you have any other favorite memories?

FA: I liked working with Richard Haydn in "I'm No Edwin Carp." Richard was a favorite of mine from films, and we got to be very good friends. I used to do an imitation of him doing an imitation of me doing an imitation of him.

TWT: Did you work with Dick on his movies?

FA: Yes, I was with him during *Mary Poppins* and *Chitty Chitty Bang Bang* and some others. I also went with him to Arizona to work on *The New Dick Van Dyke Show*. When they decided that the show was not going to continue, I told Dick I was not earning my money there with him and that I was going back to LA. I no sooner got to my home in LA when I got a call from Grant Tinker asking me to come and work for Mary.

TWT: How long did you work for Mary?

FA: I worked for Mary for about fifteen years full time and about two years part time. Mary is a "honey bear," and we were like brother and sister.

TWT: What did you do after you finished working for Mary?

FA: I opened up a shop that had antiques and some other creative items. I also did some painting and theatrical masks and made marionettes. I had the shop for about six years.

TWT: Do you have any *Dick Van Dyke Show* memorabilia?

FA: Part of my job was to buy everybody gifts. So one year, I got the score to the *Dick Van Dyke Show* theme and sent it to Europe and had music boxes made. Ironically, they're made of walnut! So I still have my music box. I don't know if anyone else still has theirs.

TWT: There's one photo of you all bandaged up in a wheelchair from the "Don't Trip Over That Mountain" episode, but you don't appear in the actual episode.

FA: I think I was in the tag. I remember at the end of the show, that darling prop man, Glenn Ross, and the whole crew left me on the stage all bound up and everybody left! But they eventually came back.

TWT: What is your most treasured moment from *The Dick Van Dyke Show*?

FA: I would be a liar if I said I had just one. There were just great moments of joy on that set. Everybody just adored everybody. I think one of the most touching times for me was when I lost my parents, and everyone rallied around me. The cast was truly my extended family. It was an experience that I will treasure forever.

Frank and I finally met during a trip of mine to Florida in 1997. Frank brought along several photos from his private archives, as well as that walnut music box that he had described previously. Although nearly thirty years old, Frank oiled up the box—and it still clicks away and plays that catchy theme song. Wouldn't I love to have that item in my private collection!

The inclusion of the Guest Star Spotlight column in the newsletter afforded me the novel opportunity to interview many talented individuals who had made a guest appearance or appearances on the show. When you review the closing credits of *The Dick Van Dyke Show*, it is amazing to note how many actors and actresses appeared on the show at the very early stages of their careers. And it's very evident that the show served as a springboard for many young actors, actresses, and comedians.

The list of other guest stars with which I have had contact is daunting. I received letters from or did interviews with performers such as Amzie Strickland (various roles), Greg Morris (known primarily as Mr. Peters but was also in "Bupkis"), Alvy Moore (various roles), Kathleen Freeman (various roles), Phil Leeds (Blackey Sorrell), Don Rickles (Lyle Delp), Dabbs Greer (various roles), Bernard Fox (various roles), Sue Ane Langdon (Marla Hendrix), William Schallert (Rev. Kirk), Lennie Weinrib (various roles), Jamie Farr (the coffee man), Van Williams (Clark Rice), Allan Melvin (Rob's army buddy and more), Sandy Kenyon (various roles), Jack Larson (Kenny Dexter), Ken Berry (Tony Daniels), Joan Staley (Valerie Blake), Michael Forest (Father Joe Coogan), Marty Ingels (Rob's Army buddy), Jackie Joseph (various roles, including the giggler), Johnny Silver (various roles), Jack Carter (Neil Schenk), Howard Morris, and Paul Winchell! What a list of stars!

Michael Forest aka Father Joe Coogan

I should point out that each of these individuals had only very positive memories to share about his or her time on *The Dick Van Dyke Show*. All noted that they were warmly welcomed by the cast and thrilled to have been part of such a marvelous experience. Many of these performers went on to have his or her own successful career—often as a result of having been involved with *The Dick Van Dyke Show*. Not a bad credit to have on your resume, would you say?

It was particularly mind-blowing for me as I interviewed these actors and actresses because I almost felt as if I were back in time, reliving each of their experiences with them as they reminisced and recalled their respective memories on *The Dick Van Dyke Show*. What a special time in classic television history!

# 13

## *The Making of "It May Look Like a Walnut"*

*The Walnut Times* got its name from the classic "It May Look Like a Walnut" episode of *The Dick Van Dyke Show*—something to which a real fan of the show immediately relates.

I had always been disappointed that this particular episode was not available for commercial sale. It is certainly the most well known and remembered episode. Is there anyone who can't recall Laura sliding down the pile of walnuts as they cascade from the living room closet?

So, I contacted Ruth Engelhardt at The William Morris Agency in Beverly Hills (Ruth has handled the affairs of CALVADA Productions for years) to inquire about the feasibility of *The Walnut Times* making "episode 51" available to fans of the show. After some negotiation, we reached an agreement in early 2000 which allowed me to produce and distribute the video.

I thought to myself…the only thing better than making the episode available would be to see if the cast members would participate in video interviews to recall their memories about the making of this episode.

I contacted the main cast members and others peripherally involved with the show. In the end, I received positive replies to participate from Carl, Dick, and Rose Marie. With commitments in place, I planned a summer 2000 trip to Los Angeles and set out to schedule specific dates and locations to conduct the interviews. In fact, it became a family adventure!

Bob Palmer confirmed that *Diagnosis Murder* would be back in production in mid-July, and that the interview could be done with Dick on the set. Perfect!

Rose Marie asked if the interview could be done at her home. Again, perfect! Rose Marie's home in the San Fernando Valley was only about ten minutes from the hospital set of *Diagnosis Murder*.

I emailed Loretta Ramos, my press contact at the Museum of Television and Radio in Beverly Hills, and inquired about the possibility of renting one of their meeting rooms to conduct the interview with Carl. Loretta quickly responded to say that the museum would be happy to provide a room for me gratis, since Carl was "a friend" of the Museum. This was just tremendous!

The interview schedule was firmed up. As it turned out, all of the interviews would be completed in the same day. First, Rose Marie's interview would be done at 11 AM. From her home, I would zip over to the *Diagnosis Murder* set to do Dick's interview about 1 PM, just as Dick wrapped up shooting for the day. Then I would travel down to the museum to interview Carl at 3 PM.

As I wrote earlier, the trip had become a family adventure, and, as such, they all went along with me as I ventured out to shoot the footage.

I arrived shortly before eleven at Rose Marie's home and parked the car on the street in front of her house. My family was going to wait for me in the car while I went inside and did the interview.

I grabbed my audio and video gear from the trunk and headed up the front walk and rang the bell. In a few moments, the door opened, and I was greeted by Rose Marie's secretary, Dodi.

"Hi. You must be David. It's nice to finally meet you in person after all the correspondence we've exchanged over the years. Come on in. Rose Marie is expecting you."

She led me to the kitchen, where Rose Marie was sitting at the kitchen table, waiting for me.

"Hello, Rose Marie. It's great to see you," I said.

"It's nice to see you again, too, David. Where would you like to set up to do the interview?" Rose Marie asked.

132   TO TWILO AND BEYOND!

As I glanced around the room, I could see a beautiful swimming pool and patio in the back yard through the kitchen windows.

"What if I set up on the patio and we talk out there?"

"Sounds fine with me," she said, as she started to get up and move toward the back door.

"And when we're all finished," I said, "I'd like to introduce you to my family if that is okay."

"Your family?" Rose Marie gave me a puzzled look. "Where is your family now?" she asked.

"They are out in the car waiting for me," I said.

With all the familiar characteristics of a Sally Rogers reply, Rose Marie stopped dead in her tracks and blurted back at me, "OUT IN THE CAR?! Go get them and invite them in here! They're not going to wait in the car."

Dodi gave a broad smile and followed me to the front door of the house as I ran out to the car to get the rest of my family.

As I finished setting up the video camera and began to conduct the interview, my wife and three children sat at the other end of the pool chatting with Dodi and snacked on freshly baked muffins and iced tea. What a fun time everyone had!

It's interesting to note that Rose Marie has several walnut trees on her property and even offered up her walnuts during the taping of the walnut episode—but prop man Glenn Ross had already taken care of "borrowing" all of them for the show.

When we finished the interview, it was about 12:30 PM, and everything was right on schedule. I packed up my equipment, we visited for a few minutes and took a couple of photos, and then we jumped in the car and were on our way to the set of *Diagnosis Murder*.

After a short ten minute drive, we pulled into the parking lot, parked the car in the rear of the building, and walked around front to go in to the main lobby area.

I announced myself to the receptionist, and she acknowledged that they were expecting me. My family and I were escorted to a section of the set where tables were all set up, and we were invited to have lunch with the rest of the cast and crew. Dick was not around at this time. He had retreated to his trailer to take a rest before shooting resumed.

Prior to my arrival, I had been told that Dick was supposed to be done for the day by no later than 1:30 PM. However, I was told that the shooting schedule was about two hours behind. As such, there would be a delay in getting started on our interview.

As we were finishing lunch, I was given permission to set up my equipment in the "operating room." I was told that Dick would come out during breaks in the shooting to do the interview. And sure enough, he appeared a few minutes later to say hello to me, meet my family, and get started on the questions which I had prepared. If you have a sharp eye, you'll notice that Dick's outfit changes during the course of the documentary—a result of the segments being shot between several different scenes of the *Diagnosis Murder* episode.

The approach of asking a few questions at a time during the breaks seemed to be working okay, but I soon realized that due to the delay in the shooting, that I was really under the gun to get Dick's interview done and still make it to Beverly Hills by 3:00 PM to conduct Carl's interview. I was so preoccupied at one point that I almost screwed up a whole segment of Dick's interview. How?

Dick had just finished a scene and came out and took a seat in a director's chair to continue where we left off in our interview. I clipped the wireless mike on his shirt as I had done several times already and stepped back across the room. I started the video camera and began my questioning. Dick had answered about three questions when it dawned on me that I had not turned the wireles microphone back on! Holy crap! I think that Dick could see the change in the expression on my face because he asked what was the matter.

"I forgot to turn the mike back on when we started this time," I explained.

"Oh. That's not good, is it?" Dick replied.

I paused the tape and quickly switched on the remote power supply for the microphone. After all the planning and coordination to make this interview a reality—what a disaster this would have been! A great video interview with Dick Van Dyke and NO sound! Fortunately, I somehow realized my deficiency and was able to correct it before it was too late. I still have that piece of video with no sound in my archives!

At this point it was painfully clear that I could not possibly make it to Beverly Hills by 3:00 PM. I made a call to Carl's office to let his assistant know that we were running a little behind. She graciously pushed the interview time back to 4:00 PM. Phew! I had been given a little breathing room.

I should probably explain at this point that Carl had not been feeling well and there was a question as to whether he would feel up to doing the interview with me during my stay. But the interview had been scheduled, and it looked like everything was falling into place.

I finished up my final few questions with Dick and thanked him for participating in the project.

"It's nice doing business with another Dutchman," he quipped.

Before he headed off, I asked if we could have a quick photo taken with my family and he obliged. Dick had been wonderful AGAIN—and especially understanding in light of my screw up with the microphone. He is one great guy!

I knew that there was not much time to get everything packed up and get down to Beverly Hills. But the rushing all became moot when I was handed a message by a staffer telling me that Carl's office had called to cancel his interview. I had lost the opportunity to interview him for the documentary.

Needless to say, I was very disappointed. At the same time, I understood entirely. Carl had not been feeling well, and the schedule had been thrown way off due to delays in the shooting. But there was nothing I could have done. It was out of my control. I reconciled myself to the fact that I would have to produce the documentary with only Rose Marie's and Dick's interviews.

I felt I should touch base with Barbara Scher to thank her for all her efforts and apologize to Carl for the scheduling problems. On the way out, I stopped in the front office to give her a call.

"Hi Barbara, it's David Van Deusen. I got your message about the canceling of Carl's interview. I wanted to call and apologize for the schedule problems, and at the same time, thank you for all of your help."

"That's show business, David," she replied. "Carl understands entirely. It was just too late in the day to get the interview done. What are you doing tomorrow?" she asked.

"Tomorrow?" I replied. I was very confused.

"Do you have time to do the interview with Carl tomorrow?"

"You mean that Carl will still do the interview with me? I thought that I had lost out!" I couldn't believe that the interview was still a possibility.

"He's available tomorrow if you can do it then."

"I just have to call the Museum and see if I can arrange for a room. I'll call you right back."

I make a feverish call to the Museum to explain what had happened and asked if they could make a room available for me the next day. Yes! They could! The interview was back on.

Originally, the family had planned to go to Disneyland the next day. I decided that I would drop the family off down in Anaheim early in the morning and return to Beverly Hills in plenty of time for my newly rescheduled 10:00 AM interview. After the interview, I would return to Disneyland to meet up with the family. Oh, what seems so simple becomes so difficult!

I had not anticipated the sheer volume of traffic that we would encounter as we headed south toward Disneyland and began to sense that I was just about going to make it back in time to do the interview. As I dropped the family off at the front gate, I asked that my wife give Barbara a call to let her know that I was on my way back from Anaheim and expected to be there in time.

I turned around and headed back toward Beverly Hills with the hope that traffic would cooperate and that I would make it in time so as to avoid COMPLETE embarrassment!

I did manage to make it back to the Museum about twenty minutes ahead of the scheduled interview time and proceeded to set up my equipment. Wow! What a whirlwind this whole event had been. And now I could finally take a breath and relax for a few minutes before Carl arrived.

Ten o'clock arrived and so did Carl with somewhat of an amusing smile on his face. He had my curiosity piqued.

"Hi, Carl," I said, as I reached and shook his hand. "Thanks for coming today. I really appreciate it."

"I hear you've been running your ass off this morning," he said with a chuckle, an obvious reference to what his assistant Barbara must have conveyed to him about my "traffic jam-plagued trip" to Anaheim and back.

"Yes," I said. "It's been quite a morning."

We both had a laugh and then each of us took a seat in chairs which I had arranged. Having learned a good lesson from the near fiasco the day before, I decided to wear a set of headphones to ensure that I was recording audio during the interview. I was ready to start.

Carl asked, "Do you want me to look at you or at the camera during the interview?"

"At me," I replied.

"Okay. Then you need to adjust your camera angle a little bit. Let me show you."

All at once it hit me. Carl Reiner was directing me on how to get the correct and best camera angle for the interview. This was tremendous!

I began the interview, and Carl shared his insights from the creator's point of view: where the original idea came from, how the storyline developed, the famous closet scene, the reaction of fans, and more.

TWT: Please tell us about how you came to write the "It May Look Like a Walnut" episode.

CR: I remember it vividly. The first year or two I think I wrote forty of the first sixty shows. I would start with a blank piece of paper, scrounge around for ideas, and see what I had to work with. In trying to write something new and different that I hadn't written before, I thought I would try to write a *Twilight Zone*-type episode, a tip of the hat to Rod Serling. And that's where I got Twilo from. The tough part was determining how you do it on The *Dick Van Dyke Show* and put Dick Van Dyke in that kind of situation. So I did it in the form of a dream. And once I got that idea, I knew I could invent a show. So I put it all together with that kind of form, and I had an awful lot of fun writing it.

TWT: How was the episode received by the cast?

CR: Everyone loved it...except for Sheldon Leonard. But Sheldon said, "It's your baby. If you want to do it, go ahead." In the end, after the episode aired, Sheldon, being the humble guy that he was, admitted that the show was very funny and that he had misread it.

TWT: How did you come up with the idea about losing your thumbs?

CR: The two things that I knew set apart man from any other animal is the sense of humor and the opposing thumb. So I gave the alien that quality. As soon as Dick read that he had no thumbs, he loved it! And it was absolutely wonderful for a comedy writer to lose his sense of humor! I knew I was home free.

TWT: Where did the idea for "four eyes" come from? You know, "20 20 20 20 vision!"

CR: Many years ago there was great black comedian who said that we were built all wrong. You should have one eye in the front and one eye in the back. You could see people coming, and, if it's good, you could keep watching without turning your head. So I figured the alien from Twilo should have two eyes in the front and two eyes in the back. The best part was that you didn't have to see the eyes to know they existed. Kolak spotted the stain on Rob's necktie, and Mary simply parted her hair a little to take a look.

TWT: What was the significance of the walnuts?

CR: There was a wonderful movie called *The Invasion of the Body Snatchers* where a pod absorbed a person's identity. So I invented a smaller version, since we only had a half hour show, and decided to use a walnut.

TWT: Do you know how many walnuts there were?

CR: There were 1800 pounds of walnuts. And we did the scene with only one rehearsal. That's all we could afford to try, since it took so long to load the closet back up.

TWT: It's rumored that the cast and crew suffered a little bit from consuming so many walnuts.

CR: It's true. Many of us got constipated!

TWT: How did you come up with some of the key phrases? Walnut roast, a nice hot bowl of walnuts...

CR: One you start writing a show and you get a premise, you run with it. And I knew every time that I could mention "walnut," it would get a laugh.

TWT: In the opening scene, Rob and Laura are watching the science fiction movie on TV. Do Dick and Mary actually see anything on the TV set?

CR: No, they were just looking at a blank screen. They could hear me as the narrator of the movie, so they could react to what I was saying, and, like all good actors, they acted like they were seeing something that was very scary.

TWT: Could they hear any of the eerie background music?

CR: No, all of the music was put in during post production.

TWT: How did Danny Thomas get involved with the episode?

CR: I wanted to give people an image of the leader from the Planet Twilo, so I said he looked like Danny Thomas but had an English accent. I thought if he looks like Danny Thomas, I bet we can get him to come in and play the role. Danny just loved the idea. And he played the part very well, too.

TWT: Did Danny get paid for his role as Kolak?

CR: Yes. First, he got paid as an owner of the show. But he also got paid for his acting...scale, I think.

TWT: Do you recall how the show was received by the audience?

CR: We got lots and lots of letters about the show. People loved it. In the mail, I received a small package with a walnut inside. The walnut had a rubber band around it. I removed the rubber band to discover that someone had put a hinge on the upper and lower part of the walnut. When you opened the nut, a little hand without a thumb popped up. And on the back of the hand, written in the smallest print, was "congratulations on one of the funniest shows I have ever seen." It was signed by Saul Bass. Saul Bass was one of the greatest Main Titlers of all time, as well as a graphics artist. He also designed some of the great logos that we still have in industry today. To receive that from Saul Bass was just a thrill. I still have it today.

TWT: How would you complete the phrase "The walnut episode was…"

CR: The walnut episode was memorable for me because it took us away from the ordinary, regular show that we normally did. It took us into a land that we didn't know about, and a kind of behavior we didn't do. When you do a dream sequence, you can do anything. And it's always a pleasure to let your mind go. So I remember it that way. I also remember it fondly because many thought it wouldn't work, and it did. Who would have ever thought there would be a newsletter named after this episode?

My final request at the end of the interview was to ask Carl if he would do his impression of Sheldon Leonard. He immediately fell into the Sheldon voice without hesitation and uttered some Leonardesque remarks. It was just great!

The interview was over, I thanked Carl, and he was gone down the hall to the elevator and out to the underground parking garage.

I paused to reflect on the events of the past couple of days and realized just how fortunate I had been to have had the opportunity to meet and interview Rose Marie, Dick, and Carl. Each of them was just wonderful and very generous with their time. These folks are truly special individuals.

Upon returning home, I began working on the script to support the interviews I had collected in LA. Shortly thereafter, I started the intense editing process to turn this raw footage into a cohesive, informative documentary about the making of this famous episode.

I was delighted to be asked to have my documentary included as bonus footage as part of *The Dick Van Dyke Show* DVD collection—and you can see it there! Thumbs up!

# 14

## *Merchandise, TV Specials, and DVDs*

The publishing of *The Walnut Times* provided a perfect mechanism for me to also get involved with other things related to the show.

One opportunity was to develop and offer some really fun merchandise. As I noted earlier, Morey worked with me to produce the Morey Amsterdam hat—and I have a fabulous photo of Morey wearing the actual hat. But I also got approval from Dick and Carl to offer some other items.

The first was *The Walnut Times* mug. This mug proudly displays a caricature drawing of the cast which was done by Dick himself during the original network run of the show. Dick says that he still has the original drawing that he did in a small little notebook.

With the manufacturing of the mug complete, I set out to also establish my own personal collection of mugs. How? As I contacted folks from the show, I asked each to autograph an individual mug for my archives—a "set" of mugs which is now a very unique collectible.

My initial visit to the set of *Diagnosis Murder* had yielded some terrific photos for me to use in the newsletter—including a single shot of Dick holding the giant walnut. With a little imagination (yes, I still had my thumbs) and some creativity, I thought that one of the photos would be a great image to depict on the face of a wristwatch. And so was created the Walnut Times watch, featuring a great color image of Dick. Dick thought the watch was just a great idea!

Merchandise, TV Specials, and DVDs   143

*The Walnut Times* mug—Caricature drawing by Dick Van Dyke

October 2001 marked the 40th anniversary of the debut of *The Dick Van Dyke Show*, and I felt that this occasion should be noted with some kind of special recognition. I again engaged the services of John Graziano, a fantastic artist, who had done some wonderful artwork for me previously—including the great caricature of Dick with the spinning walnut, giving the thumbs up sign.

I described the concept that I had in mind for what would ultimately be described as *The Dick Van Dyke Show* 40th Anniversary print.

I told John that I wanted to have a drawing of everyone in the Petrie living room, as if they had all gathered to celebrate this anniversary. The drawing should include Rob, Laura, Ritchie, Buddy, Sally, Mel, Alan Brady, and Jerry and Millie. The drawing should also include some other important figures in the history of *The Dick Van Dyke Show*—Kolak, Big Max Calvada, and one other party guest. I'm not sure what name of the character would be in this case, but I am sure that the role was played by Frank Adamo!

John took my idea and ran with it to create a phenomenal drawing to commemorate this distinguished milestone. I was thrilled to publish the artwork in a special edition of the newsletter, and also sent copies of the print to several of the cast and crew members from the show.

The Dick Van Dyke Show 40th Anniversary print

The next item, and perhaps the most original piece of memorabilia to be created, was *The Dick Van Dyke Show* collectible print.

This unique portrait contains a variety of photos and objects. Some of these represent characters from the show, while others have relevance to a particular episode from the show. Take a close look. Do the objects in the photo jog your memory of a favorite or classic moment from *The Dick Van Dyke Show*? A glass doorknob? A one-of-a-kind brooch? A bowling pin? A toupee? How many objects can you recognize and associate with specific episodes? Over thirty episodes are depicted in this exclusive print—an extraordinary way to celebrate and honor *The Dick Van Dyke Show*.

*The Dick Van Dyke Show* Collectible montage
Photo by Lloyd Aadland Photography

The final merchandise item that was developed was a walnut themed t-shirt. Fans always seem to love a t-shirt related to their favorite show. And although there had been a few t-shirt offerings of *The Dick Van Dyke Show* in the mid 1990s, they were not widely available for some reason. Again, I turned to artist John Graziano and described my idea of the artwork that I wanted to present on the t-shirt.

I told John that I wanted the drawing to include Rob, Sally, and Buddy. Further, I described that Rob should have "no thumbs," Sally should be giving a "thumbs up," and Buddy should be holding a particle of absorbitron in one hand while juggling walnuts with the other. As you can see, the final product was just outstanding—and a real hit with fans!

Caricature drawing by John Graziano

Another opportunity which presented itself to me as result of publishing the newsletter was to act as a consultant about Dick Van Dyke and *The Dick Van Dyke Show* to various entities. Due to my vast knowledge of the show, as well as the extensive collection of photos and memorabilia, I have often been contacted to provide input and information about the show.

My first significant contribution was to provide reference photos of Dick as Rob Petrie for a statue commissioned by the Academy of Television Arts & Sciences relative to Dick's earlier induction into the Television Hall of Fame. Not only did I provide photos to sculptor Thomas Marsh for his use as source material in creating the full figure statue, I was also on hand for the official unveiling of the artwork at the Disney-MGM Studios in September 1998. Stacy Van Dyke accepted on behalf of her dad.

E! Entertainment was the first company to approach me to help with a celebrity profile that they were producing about Dick Van Dyke.

It just so happened that I was going to be in LA for a visit when E! was shooting its footage for their special.

I did an extensive interview and loaned a myriad of photos from my collection. I also brought along a *Walnut Times* coffee mug with Dick's drawing of the cast.

Well, does it surprise you that my interview footage never made it to the special? That's right. Every piece of it hit the cutting room floor. The producer claimed he had too much material and my interview segment was the first to go!

Actually, I did make it into the program—sort of. You can see my hand holding the *Walnut Times* coffee mug in the very opening segment! And they did give me a small credit at the end of the show. That's Hollywood for you, I guess.

The next company to contact me was Peter Jones Productions. Jones was producing a two hour A&E Biography on Dick Van Dyke. I worked closely with Selina Lin, the producer, and provided background information and many photos from my archives.

This was a much different experience than the first. First, I was treated in a much more professional way. Second, the show was extremely well done—a notch or two above your typical program. And last, Ms. Lin was nice enough to provide me with a complimentary copy of the program for my archives. Very nice!

To top it off, I was ecstatic to discover that a photo of Dick and me sitting together that I had provided had made it into the final cut of the biography. I believe the inclusion of this photo was a very nice gesture of thanks from Selina for all of my help and efforts on the special.

The final documentary program that I had involvement with was *Inside TV Land—The Dick Van Dyke Show*—a program which was produced for TV Land. At this stage in the life of the newsletter, my reputation as somewhat of an expert about the show was widely known, and the staff involved with the show located me early on during the production to see what help I might be able to provide.

I provided extensive contact information for many of the people who were involved with the show. I even suggested peripheral cast and crew members who I thought could provide some interesting insights—people the producers did not even know existed or knew were still alive.

I loaned my extensive collection of both color and black and white photographs, and contributed some little known trivia about the show that I thought would provide some interesting information for fans of the show.

As the exchange of information was ongoing, I was formally asked to travel to New York City to do an in-person interview. I would provide the point of view of the fan—something that is a little different than what is traditionally included in a retrospective program about a classic television show.

I did go to New York and the interview went extremely well. I felt very good about the perspective I offered about my favorite show! In fact, my interview was so extensive that it spanned two videocassettes. Initial feedback I received about the content of my interview from the associate producer soon after my return home was very favorable.

This program surely had the potential to be one of the very best programs ever done about *The Dick Van Dyke Show*, and I was very excited about contributing to and being included in this special. I was even advised that the program length had been extended from one hour to 1½ hours because the producers had accumulated so much interesting and new material. This boosted my confidence level that my interview—in some shape or form—would make it to the final cut. You see, after my negative experience with E!, I had been somewhat cautious and apprehensive about participating on this special. But I had developed a very good feeling about this show.

Well, what can I say? Don't trust your feelings. Approximately six weeks prior to the scheduled airdate, nearly two months after my interview had been conducted, I received the dreaded phone call.

The associate producer called to tell me that no part of my interview would be included in the program. I was stunned.

"It won't be included?" I asked. "Can you tell me why?"

"Something happened to the tape that your interview was recorded on and none of the footage is usable," the producer explained.

It didn't make sense to me. "Something was wrong with the tape?" I inquired.

"Yes," she replied. "Apparently the tape was defective."

I couldn't believe what I was hearing. How could this be? Was it possible that I had been hoodwinked again? It took me only a moment to realize that the answer to this question was an undeniable YES!

As the producer continued to plead her case, I flashed back in my mind to the hotel room where the interview had been held and recalled distinctly that my interview had spanned TWO videotapes. Was it likely that both tapes were bad or defective? What do you think? I think not!

"Are you telling me that both of the videotapes from my interview were defective?" I inquired with a considerable bit of assertion in my voice.

There was a major pause on the other end of the line followed by a somewhat timid reply.

"Both tapes?" she asked. "What do you mean?"

I proceeded to explain that my interview had gone so long that it had spanned two videocassettes.

"I find it very difficult to believe that both videotapes of my interview were defective. And I know that Mary's interview was conducted after mine. Was her videotape okay?"

"Well, yes," she responded. "Her interview came out fine."

Hmmm. Imagine that! My tape was totally defective, but Mary's came out okay—even though they were conducted one right after the other.

And of course, at this point, I had given the producers invaluable information about the show and cast which they had used to develop the content and direction of this special. I had also provided full access to my large repository of photos and collectibles for inclusion in the show.

I could surely smell a rat. It was very apparent that I had caught the producer with her pants down—and at this point, she did not know what to say.

"Why can't you just be honest with me?" I asked. "Just tell me that you've decided you're not going to include my footage. And I'll be angry, but at least you will have been forthright with me!"

Again, there was somewhat of a pause and not much of a response. I had caught her so off guard, she didn't know what to say or how to respond. I recall making my feeling pretty clear and then the conversation ended shortly thereafter.

The documentary premiered a few weeks later on TV Land and was extremely well received. Truthfully, I think it is probably the best retrospective ever done on *The Dick Van Dyke Show*.

Despite the fact that I was clearly taken advantage of, I'd like to think that the superb quality of the program was in many ways related to the fact that I was involved at some level—giving access to my photo collection (of which nearly 30 photos were ultimately woven into the special)—and providing information and thought provoking remarks which possibly acted as fodder for questions that were ultimately asked during interviews of the cast members. And I guess that I was subtly assuaged by the fact that I did get a credit or two at the end of the show, too.

My most recent and last involvement as a researcher and consultant related to *The Dick Van Dyke Show* was when I was asked to be involved with the effort to release the show on DVD.

The contact came from Paul Brownstein Productions who had been contracted by The William Morris Agency/Calvada Productions to coordinate and produce the issuance of the show in association with Image Entertainment. My involvement with this project was tri-fold.

First, interest was expressed to include my walnut documentary as bonus footage in the Season Two compilation. Absolutely! It would be a thrill to have my creative efforts shared with all other *Dick Van Dyke Show* fans.

Second, I was asked to lend my entire collection of photos and other significant show memorabilia for inclusion in a Photo Gallery area on the DVD. Including still photos on the DVDs was a somewhat new approach for bonus material, but this idea was ultimately very well received. In addition to providing access to my photos, I was asked to identify what specific episodes were represented by particular photos so that these photos could be appropriately linked to the associated season sets.

Third, I was asked to provide my input as to what I believed would be interesting bonus footage for fans of the show. I made several recommendations and suggestions, all of which were given serious consideration. Having been a fan of the show for many years, I was aware of a great deal of related show footage that I knew existed somewhere out there—and would be just marvelous if it could be located and included.

I was personally interested in finding interview footage which was shot in 1994 when *The Dick Van Dyke Show Remembered* program was produced. Although in-depth interviews were conducted with all living cast members (which included both Morey Amsterdam and Sheldon Leonard at that time), the final program which aired on CBS contained only minimal amounts of these cast member insights.

Both Rose Marie and Morey Amsterdam had conveyed to me that each cast member had done a one hour interview individually, and that many cast members were then also interviewed together. I knew that there had to be some great content in these interviews.

Although these cast interviews could not be found initially, continued digging resulted in the unearthing of this rare and invaluable footage—much of which eventually ended up as great bonus material on the DVDs! What a treasure for fans of the show!

*The Dick Van Dyke Show* DVD collection has truly set the standard of quality for what is now expected when a television show is released on DVD. From the digital transfer of the original 35mm film prints, to the inclusion of fabulous bonus footage and a unique show Photo Gallery, to the slick and classy packaging—*The Dick Van Dyke Show* DVD collection is one that we fans are fortunate to have and will be able to truly appreciate for generations to come!

# 15

## *The TV LAND Awards*

It was the middle of February in 2003, and I was doing some browsing on the Internet when I came upon a press release which announced the first Annual TV Land Awards. TV Land Awards? What was this all about?

A closer read indicated that the event, sponsored by TV Land, would recognize shows and stars from television's rich history which have withstood the test of time. The release further revealed that *The Dick Van Dyke Show* would be honored with the top honor of the night—the TV Legend Award. The gala event, including red carpet introductions, would be held March 2, 2003, at the historic Hollywood Palladium theatre on Sunset Boulevard in Hollywood. And Carl, Dick, Mary, Rose Marie, and Larry would all be there to accept the award!

I briefly envisioned being in the press contingent covering the event to get some photos of the cast members as they came down the red carpet. That would be tremendous. My thoughts continued. But let's be realistic. The event was less than ten days away. Could I possibly even get press credentials? Even if I could get credentials, could I make travel arrangements that would not be cost prohibitive given such short notice?

I told a co-worker that I was thinking about going to the event. His response? What was there to think about? This could potentially be the last time that the cast would all be together. There was no question that I had to go.

I shot an email to my press contact at TV Land to inquire about the possibility of getting press credentials. Within an hour's time, I had received an email back stating that I was "good to go." With that hurdle out of the way, I moved forward to investigating potential travel arrangements.

Somehow I managed to get a flight whose cost was not exorbitant. I would leave New York late on Saturday and arrive in LA around 8:00 PM. I would attend the event the next day and return home to New York on Monday.

My plane flights went without a hitch. It was now Sunday, and I was supposed to be at the Press Tent about 1:30 PM to get my credentials. Keep in mind that, at this point in time, all I had clearance for was to cover the red carpet arrivals as a member of the press. I was not an invited guest to the actual awards show, nor did I have a ticket to get into the event.

I arrived about 1:20 PM and checked in. I was on the official list to cover the event. As other members of the video and photo press arrived, I began to sense that they were all looking at me and wondering who I was. You see, all of the photographers know each other from covering the many different events in Hollywood. Apparently, they all recognized me as an outsider.

Shortly before 3:30 PM, we were escorted to an area on one side of the red carpet to position ourselves for the soon to be arriving celebrities. Due to the luck of the draw, I managed to snatch a prime spot along the railing for getting good shots of the arrivals.

It was pretty exciting. On the other side of the red carpet was a bleacher full of classic TV fans, ready to welcome their favorite characters from the TV shows they loved.

The members of *The Dick Van Dyke Show* cast arrived at various intervals during the red carpet ceremony. The first to arrive was Larry Mathews, along with his wife, Jennifer.

As he came down the runway and approached my location, I called out to him from behind the railing.

"Hey, Larry!" I shouted for him to hear me over the screaming fans. He turned my way and spotted me in the crowd.

"David! You made it!" he said. I had sent an email to Larry to let him know that I was going to try to come to the event but wasn't sure if it would happen.

With that recognition, Larry came over and shook my hand and introduced me to his wife, Jennifer. They stepped back and I was able to get a couple of great shots of the couple. Then, they were on their way.

At the same time, I could feel the looks of the other photographers that surrounded me. Who is this guy? How come Larry Mathews came over to him and shook his hand?

The next cast member to come down the carpet was Rose Marie. I had also sent Rose Marie's daughter a quick email to let her know that I might be coming.

"Hey, Rose Marie!"

She glanced in my direction and found me amongst the herd of photographers.

"You are just amazing," she exclaimed, as she continued toward me and gave me a big hug and a kiss. Again, I could feel the eyes of the other members of the press staring at me. "I'm so glad you're here!"

Other stars from classic television steadily arrived and proceeded down the red carpet past the Batmobile, the Clampett's jalopy, and the Munster buggy through the giant, television shaped entrance to the theatre. This was going to be one huge event.

Remaining cast members Dick Van Dyke, Mary Tyler Moore, and Carl Reiner all arrived within minutes of each other and were also greeted with roars of appreciation from the crowd. As they came down the red carpet, I was stunned at how the photographers were calling out to them, almost demanding that they look in their direction so they could obtain the perfect "head on" shot.

The press had been told that, when the show started, they would be escorted back to a tent at the rear of the property where they would be able to watch the show on a closed circuit feed from inside the theatre. As celebrities were acknowledged and given awards, they would be shown to the press tent where photos could be taken of them with their awards.

(top) Carl Reiner with wife, Estelle Reiner

While that set up seemed good to me initially, now I really wanted to get inside of the theatre to see the show as a member of the audience. The show was to start at 5:00 PM, and it was almost 4:15 PM.

As I began to ponder what I might do to try to get inside, I spotted Larry Jones, General Manager of TV Land, walking down the opposite side of the red carpet.

Larry and I had never met each other in person, yet we knew each other pretty well from phone calls and correspondence that had been exchanged, and Larry was well aware of *The Walnut Times*. I called out to him from behind the railing.

"Larry!" I shouted. He turned in my direction. "Can I introduce myself to you?" I asked.

With that he stopped and approached me.

"I'm David Van Deusen from *The Walnut Times*," I said.

"Hey, David! It's nice to finally meet you in person and it's great that you're here. And your show is going to win the big award tonight."

"I hope so," I replied.

"You hope so?" Larry chuckled. "I can tell you without questions that they're going to win it."

Here was my chance to take a shot and see what would happen.

"But I don't have a ticket to get inside and see them receive the award," I explained. "I know the show is going to start in just a little while, but is there any way I can possibly get inside? I'll understand if it's too late, but I didn't know I was coming out here until a couple of days ago."

"Let me see what I can do." With that, Larry took out his cell phone and started to make a call. In the midst of his conversation, he was summoned away to attend to another matter, so I had no idea what was the outcome of his call. As he continued to talk on the phone, he turned and waved to me.

What did that mean, I wondered? Did that mean I was going to be able to get into the show or not? I had no idea.

I continued to take photos of the few late arriving celebrities as I waited with anticipation to see if some arrangement had been made.

As I finished shooting a photo, my eye caught two TV Land staffers on the other side of the carpet motioning toward me and pointing.

The man saw me looking at him and mouthed the words, "Are you David?"

"Yes," I said, nodding my head up and down at the same time.

He approached me with an envelope and handed it to me. "This is from Larry," he said. "It's your ticket to get into the show."

"Excellent! Thanks a lot!" I said. I closed up my camera and picked up the pace of my step as I headed for the entrance. I couldn't wait to get inside.

I handed my ticket to the girl at the door and was asked to surrender my camera at coat check. I didn't care if I could take pictures. I was inside to see the show!

The main room was filled with round tables of nine seats each. Because the cast was receiving the "big" award of the night, they and their guests were seated at two tables, front and center in the ballroom. My ticket and assigned seat was for a table near the rear of the room on a subtly elevated level.

I found my seat and sat down. The show would be starting very soon. In a way, I felt a little guilty. It seemed like the other people seated at my table were employees of TV Land—and I suspected that I had probably taken a seat away from one of the staffers.

Within a few minutes, the program began with an awesome medley of classic TV theme songs. You'll recall from earlier chapters that I had written an arrangement of The Dick Van Dyke Show theme for Dick for his 75th birthday at the time before he had actually established his singing group. You'll also recall that I had read that Dick and his group had been performing *The Dick Van Dyke Show* theme at various events, but Dick's publicist had told me that the arrangement they were singing had been written by one of the members of his group.

The opening medley continued. Enter Dick Van Dyke and the Vantastix for the singing of *The Dick Van Dyke Show* theme. As the performance began, it immediately grabbed my attention. Wait! What was I hearing? The arrangement they were singing sounded to me like the one that I had written! Was that possible? Could Dick's publicist have been mistaken? Had they been singing my arrangement all along without me knowing it?

As I attempted to make sense of what was transpiring, Dick and the group finished their segment and were on their way off the stage. The performance was tremendous. What a way to start the show! I would have to follow up somehow to confirm that they were performing my arrangement. But the more I replayed the song in my head, I was convinced that it was the arrangement that I had written.

The Awards program continued and was truly a blast down television memory lane, and, as such, the room was filled with a plethora of classic television personalities. Several honors were bestowed as the evening progressed with the top award of the night to be given to *The Dick Van Dyke Show* cast. This award had been labeled as the TV Legend Award.

Ted Danson and Matthew Perry had been tapped as presenters of the Legend Award to the cast. Danson gave some opening remarks and commented about how much he enjoyed having Dick guest star with him on his TV sitcom, *Becker*. A variety of memorable clips from *The Dick Van Dyke Show* were displayed on the giant TV screen mounted on the stage, including, of course, the famous pouring out of walnuts and Laura Petrie from the living room closet. Perry was introduced by Danson, and Matthew invited the cast members to the stage to receive their award.

As the band began to play *The Dick Van Dyke Show* theme music and the cast members approached the stage, I rose to my feet to give the cast a standing ovation. The rest of the audience also quickly responded with cheers and applause and rose to its feet as well. After quite some time, when the applause finally died down, Dick offered the first remarks. Dick noted that the creation and making of *The Dick Van Dyke Show* was a very special time in all of their lives, and the cast knew even then that it was something very unique. He also gave credit to the genius of Carl Reiner for the success of the show. His comments were followed with additional thoughts by Mary, Rose Marie, Larry, and, finally, Carl.

Rose Marie offered a special tribute to Morey Amsterdam, commenting that he was her dearest friend and that "if Morey were here tonight, he'd have done twenty minutes. This [award] is for you Morey!"

In addition to the thanks offered to Carl Reiner, Larry Mathews also gave recognition to Executive Producer Sheldon Leonard for the opportunity that Sheldon had provided to him.

Carl stepped to the microphone and joked that this Awards show was really weird—kind of like from the *Twilight Zone*. Hmmm…a little throw back to the "Twilo" zone, perhaps? He further remarked that Larry Jones and TV Land were very smart to create such a "light" award, since everyone was getting older and wouldn't be able to carry anything too heavy! Finally, Carl announced that he was considering writing a *Dick Van Dyke Show* situation comedy reunion script which would bring together all of the living cast members—if the cast would agree to return for the reunion.

Dick announced that the words to *The Dick Van Dyke Show* theme were written by none other than Morey Amsterdam and Carl asked Dick to sing it again, which he did, so that everyone could have a better chance to hear Morey's words!

As this portion of the show unfolded, I just sat there and soaked all of it up. I was very, very glad that I had made the decision to travel to Los Angeles for this event. It had been an incredible experience, with all the living cast members together. I was especially happy that I had taken the initiative to call out and introduce myself to Larry Jones. Otherwise, I would have been relegated to the press tent instead of being able to enjoy the show from inside the theater.

Final remarks were offered, and the awards show came to a close. The audience again acknowledged the indelible impression that *The Dick Van Dyke Show* had left for so many years by joining together in yet another standing ovation.

At this point, the cast was heading toward an exit door at the back of the stage and to the press tent for photos and interviews.

I jumped from my seat, retrieved my camera from coat check, and dashed out the door, back up the red carpet to the press tent. I managed to beat the cast there by a minute or two.

As the cast posed for the press core in the main tent, I took advantage of the opportunity to shoot several photos. After a few minutes, they were all escorted around the corner to the private TV Land press tent for photos.

I exited the rear of the main tent in an effort to catch up with cast and say hello. I spotted Rose Marie as she spotted me, and she waved me toward her.

"Come on with me," she said. "We're going to the TV Land tent to take some more photos."

I immediately joined Rose Marie in the short walk toward the other tent. As we arrived at the entrance, Larry Mathews also showed up. I stayed back as they started to go inside.

"What are you doing?" she asked. "You're with me. You can come inside."

I did, in fact, go inside and took a couple of pictures of Rose Marie and Larry—and also asked Larry to take one of Rose Marie and me.

I could see that the TV Land photographer was just about ready to shoot the official photos so I discreetly slipped outside the tent to wait for them to finish.

Outside the tent entrance, I came upon Bob Palmer, Dick's publicist, and the other members of Dick's quartet. Bob introduced me to the group, and we talked briefly about their singing of the theme song. They were all very nice. One of the guys, Mike Mendyke, told me that the group had been working on an audio CD of songs. We exchanged email addresses so I could contact him at a later time for more information. I did not get into a discussion about who had written the vocal arrangement that had been performed, but I thought Mike might be the guy to confirm it for me at a later time. But more and more, I believed that it was mine.

While we were all talking, Dick and Carl had slipped by us into an adjacent tent to do a short video interview. When they finished, they came out together. Bob called out to Dick to tell him that I had made the trip from New York for the show so we could say hello. Dick was as nice as ever. Bob's gesture also drew Reiner's attention to me.

"You're here?" Carl asked. "I didn't know you were coming."

"I didn't know I was coming either," I replied, "until this past Wednesday, Carl. But how could I not come and miss all of this?" Carl gave me a broad smile and started back toward the theater. With all the "business" out of the way, it was now time for the post awards party.

"Would you like to join Rose Marie and her family and me and my wife at our table for the party?" It was Larry Mathews.

"Absolutely!" I responded. "I'll be back inside in a couple of minutes to join you." I took a few more candid photos of the cast before returning inside to partake in the festivities.

At the party, I had another opportunity or two to talk with Dick and Carl, and even ran into Sam Denoff to say hello. I then spent the remainder of the evening with Larry, his wife, Jennifer, and Rose Marie and her daughter, Georgiana, and Georgiana's husband, Steve. Amidst the frequent visits by other celebrities and the occasional request for an autograph, we had a wonderful evening of good food and delightful conversation.

As the party began to wind down, Rose Marie's daughter, Georgiana, leaned over to tell me that they were going to head out. I decided that I should probably get going as well. I got up from my seat and approached Rose Marie.

"I understand you're on your way out," I said. "Could I possibly escort you to your car?" I asked.

Rose Marie turned and gave me a big grin. "That would be wonderful," she said.

We retrieved our belongings and made our way out of the theatre and up the hallway to the main entrance. As I accompanied her toward the door, our conversation reflected on what a remarkable evening it had been. You can say that again!

Five days prior to this day, I didn't even know what a TV Land Award was. I had originally traveled to California to be a press photographer at the event yet somehow had managed to wheedle my way inside of the theater to attend the show as a guest. Then, I was witness to Dick Van Dyke and his group performing what I believed was my vocal arrangement of *The Dick Van Dyke Show* theme song in front of a live audience for broadcast on national television. My experience had continued as I watched *The Dick Van Dyke Show* cast be honored as TV Legends, and then I was able to join in a party with the cast members from my all time favorite television show. And finally, I was now escorting Rose Marie, our "Sally Rogers," to her waiting, chauffer-driven automobile. Yes! What a remarkable evening it had been!

As Rose Marie got into her car, I wished her and her family well.

"I'm looking forward to seeing your photos," she said. "Be sure to send some to me. And have a safe trip home. We'll talk again soon."

I returned home to New York the following day with a fabulous collection of photos which have now joined my permanent archive of *Dick Van Dyke Show* memorabilia.

Shortly after my return, I did contact Mike Mendyke, one of the members of Dick's quartet, by email and asked if he knew who had written the arrangement of the theme that they had performed.

"I'm afraid that I don't know any of the details of who arranged it," wrote Mike, "although I imagine that information is on the sheet music. But I actually don't seem to have a copy of the sheet music. I think we all learned it off of Dick's only copy, quickly memorized it, and never bothered to pass copies around. I'll check with Dick and see what I can find out."

A few days later, I received another email from Mike.

"Well, what do you know?" he wrote. "I borrowed Dick's copy of the theme song during rehearsal yesterday, and it turns out that it is, indeed, your arrangement. We did modify it just a bit to make it our own but it's really mostly yours!"

Very cool!

# 16

## *The Dick Van Dyke Show Revisited*

My one and only disappointment about *The Dick Van Dyke Show* and my publishing of *The Walnut Times* is that I was not old enough at the time of the show's network run to have been able to attend a filming of an episode. How cool it would have been to be a part of the audience at Desilu Cahuenga and experience "first hand" the creative atmosphere that must have existed at that time. I can only imagine what it would have been like to watch this incredible cast performing on those very distinctive home and office sets. So, when the possibility of a reunion show was seriously being given consideration, I was positively elated! I might get to fulfill "my dream" after all.

As I noted earlier, although TV Land claims that the idea for the *Dick Van Dyke Show* reunion was born at the first annual TV Land Awards in March 2003, I can state unequivocally that Carl had started to write the script for the *Revisited* show several months before.

That said, I will concede that Carl's idea certainly drew much greater attention when he asked the cast in front of a live audience (and who knows how many viewers on television) if they would be part of his project. What could they say?

It is interesting to consider the fact that Carl had been pursued for years by CBS to do some kind of reunion show but had always resisted with the sentiment that "you can't go home again."

In the early 1990s, Carl was interviewed on *Larry King Live* and made the statement that he was wondering whatever happened to Rob and Laura Petrie—and maybe he would have to sit down and write a few pages. Like many fans, I was very excited to even hear the hint of a possible update or reunion and shot off a letter to Carl to encourage him with his idea. Nothing ever transpired as a result of his comments.

The months passed after Carl's announcement on TV Land with no definitive news, but I continued to stay in touch with Barbara Scher at Carl's office to see if any firm deals had been made or plans finalized.

Production of the reunion show was initially considered for August of 2003 and then pushed back to late fall of 2003. But the fall date came and went without any concrete plans. I got a sinking feeling in the pit of my stomach that the show might never happen.

With the start of the new year, I contacted Barbara again to see if any new information about the show had become available—and indeed there was! She explained that there were many details yet to be negotiated, but it looked like production would take place sometime in March. I immediately composed a letter to Carl which expressed my interest in attending the rehearsals and taping, as well as my desire to cover the show from a "behind the scenes" perspective for *The Walnut Times*.

Carl responded to me and indicated that he greatly appreciated my enthusiasm but felt it would not be feasible for me to be on the set during rehearsal week. It would be far too chaotic. At the same time, Carl noted that he would be very happy to have me attend the live taping of the show at the end of the week.

As March approached I was in frequent contact with Carl's office to confirm the finalized production dates. Due to the many details and complex scheduling involved in a production of this magnitude, the actual production dates continued to be shifting and elusive. As such, I had not been able to make definitive travel arrangements for the trip from New York to Los Angeles.

The first week of March arrived, and I sent a note to confirm the finalized date of the taping and ask if I was still welcome to be a part of the live audience.

Barbara quickly responded to me to explain that a finalized date was still not confirmed, and there was a good possibility that the show would not be done in front of a live audience. Instead, it might be done "block and shoot"—over the course of three days, without an audience.

My heart sunk. Since Carl had indicated I would be welcome to attend the live taping of the show—and now there might not be a live taping. What did that mean to my being able to be a part of this very special reunion? At this point, it was just a little more than a week until the tentatively planned shooting schedule.

I sent an email back asking Barbara if I would still be welcome to come if the show was not ultimately going to be performed in front of a live audience. I provided my home phone number, my cell phone number, and my work phone number to ensure she had every possible way to contact me. A short time later, a return email dropped into my mailbox.

I winced as I opened it, hoping that it would not contain the bad news I knew was a distinct possibility.

"Call me tomorrow afternoon," said the note from Scher. "I hope to have more information for you by then."

PHEW! She didn't say I COULDN'T come! It looked like my hopes were still alive.

The next day I called Barbara as she had instructed to find out if Carl had given his okay for me to attend.

"I'm sorry to say that I don't have any more news for you," she explained. "Carl has been very busy with all of the details related to the show, and I haven't had a chance to talk with him about your coming. I will leave a note tonight along with the thirty or so others that I already have for him. Give me a call tomorrow, and, hopefully, I'll be able to give an answer."

I thanked Barbara for all of her help and told her I would give a call back the next day. It was now only one week prior to the shooting date.

I retreated to my home office to tend to some email. A short time later, as I was wading through the list of email, my cell phone rang. As I answered the call, I glanced at the display to observe that it was a "private" incoming number.

"Hello?"

"David?" the voice inquired. "It's Carl Reiner."

Carl Reiner? Calling me on my cell phone? I was taken aback.

"Hi, Carl," I responded. "What's up?"

"Do you want to come out to LA for this show?" he asked.

"Absolutely," I blurted back. "It would be great."

"Can you be a fly on the wall?" asked Reiner.

"I can be whatever you want me to be Carl."

"Okay then," he said. "Come on out! You can sit up in the bleachers and watch the taping. And if you see something funny, you can laugh too! Maybe you'll even end up as part of the laugh track."

"Thanks, Carl. I'll see you next week."

I was just ecstatic! What a tremendous opportunity for me. I hung up the phone and immediately began to make my final travel arrangements. And before I knew it, a week had elapsed, and I was on my way to LA.

As I drove up to the security gate at the CBS Studio City lot, I somehow almost couldn't believe that I was really there. I gave my name to the guard.

"Yes sir," she said, "you are on the list."

"The list," I said to myself. "I am on the list!"

I parked my car in the garage and grabbed my gear. Off to Stage 16, the home of *The Dick Van Dyke Show Revisited* and next door to the current soundstage of *Will and Grace.*

As I entered the soundstage on the first day of shooting, it was a flurry of activity. Cameras were being positioned, and lighting was being adjusted. I climbed the stairs to the bleachers. There were only a handful of people in the stands. I dropped my bag in the back row of seats and walked down to the front of the bleachers to scope out the sets.

The first thing that caught my eye was the recreated set of the Petrie living room—IN COLOR! The set looked identical to the original and the attention to detail was amazing. There were four other sets on the soundstage: a music studio, two other living rooms, and a kitchen. Hmmm...how would these be used in the story? As I looked around, it became quickly apparent that they were about to do some rehearsing, so I quickly made my way back up into the bleachers.

As I panned the soundstage, Larry Mathews walked out onto the Petrie living room set. I could overhear some people talking in front of me and quickly realized that these folks were Larry's dad and mom.

Larry started to rehearse some of his lines and with that, there was a response from offstage. The voice was clearly recognizable as that of Carl Reiner. The dialogue continued. When they finished the scene, Larry brought Carl over to say hello to his parents.

Carl then moved to the center of the set to consult with long time writers/producers Sam Denoff and Bill Persky. Sam and Bill had returned as story consultants to be part of this very unique production. I had never met Bill, so I was optimistic that I would finally get the opportunity.

Glancing around the rest of the set, I observed that each of the cast members had a director's chair with his or her name on it, in classic *Dick Van Dyke Show* logo lettering. Rose Marie later commented that everything had fallen right back into place, and it was as if the cast just picked right up where they left off nearly forty years before.

As scenes were rehearsed and performed, you could hear laughs coming from the folks who were seated in the bleachers—especially when a line or two was goofed up or someone decided to improvise. Carl encouraged those in the bleachers to go ahead and laugh, as the mikes over the audience bleachers were live and recording the responses. It was amazing just to sit and watch this ensemble of classic performers working together again. The mood was very laid back as was evidenced by the fact that, between scenes, Dick would sometimes be singing a little or dancing a little. At the same time, everyone was extremely attentive and immersed in the dynamics of the scene at hand.

During breaks, I talked to some of the cast members about the set recreation of the Petrie living room. Larry Mathews commented that the set was virtually identical to the original set (except it seemed a lot bigger when he was a kid!) Mary Tyler Moore remarked that coming back on the set was like being on an episode of *The Twilight Zone*. Writer/producer Sam Denoff also agreed that the living room was exactly as he remembered it some forty years ago. I also spoke with the Production Set Designers to ask what process they used to rebuild this famous room.

With Barbara Scher, Carl Reiner's assistant

With Sam Denoff and Bill Persky

It was interesting to find out that they reviewed large amounts of footage from the original show as well as numerous photographs. Ultimately, it was decided what exact furniture would be included (since the living room décor changed over time during the course of the show).

The couch that was used in the living room was custom made for the show, since a suitable one could not be found for purchase. The painting of horses on the living room wall near the couch was digitally recreated by artists so it would match as closely as possible. Brand new replicas of the two paintings on the rear wall of the living room were painted by an artist after screen captures were provided for reference. The set designers also believed that one of the living room lamps and the bar stools were actually the set pieces used on the original show. Truly amazing!

I should point out that not only was this production a reunion of the original cast members from the show but it was also a reunion of many of the children of these performers, many of whom had not seen each other in several years.

On the set to observe the production were Dick's daughters, Stacy and Carrie, and Rose Marie's daughter, Georgiana. Georgiana and Stacy were the best of friends as young adults and shared a common interest in horses. Rob Reiner and sister Ann also stopped by the set for a visit.

Do you remember that Ann Guilbert was expecting in the early years of the series? Well, both of Ann's daughters came to the set with their children—and one of the daughters was the daughter born during the show. Interestingly, this daughter is actress Hallie Todd, most recently known as the mom on Disney's popular *Lizzie McGuire* series.

Julie Paris, daughter of the late Jerry Paris, also came by to say hello. Larry Mathews recalled that Julie and each of their siblings used to get together frequently at each other's houses. What memories!

Paul Idelson, Bill's son, who, you will recall, grew up down the street from Julie and her brothers, was also enjoying watching the shooting of the show and reminiscing about the wonderful times they had had as kids. This show was truly a reunion from many different perspectives!

I watched with great interest as day one of production progressed. When the shooting broke at mid-day, I joined Larry Mathews and his family for lunch at a nearby restaurant. Larry commented that the experience had been wonderful so far! Even the rehearsal week had been a lot of fun.

As the end of day one approached, Ray Romano arrived to shoot the opening and closing segments for the show. Mary and Dick were dressed to the hilt for the closing scene in the living room, wearing an evening gown and tuxedo respectively. They rehearsed the scene a couple of times and then took a break.

All of a sudden, there was considerable commotion on the living room set and everyone's attention was drawn over to that part of the soundstage.

(top) Larry Mathews with Rose Marie's daughter, Georgiana
(bottom) Larry Mathews with Julie Paris

Hallie Todd with mom, Ann Guilbert

There stood Rob Reiner alongside Mary Tyler Moore. As a hush fell over the group, the next thing we heard was the director call out "Action!"

Rob proceeded to talk to Mary and the audience about *The Dick Van Dyke Show* urban legend that claimed that Rob had pinched Mary's behind when he was about sixteen years old.

Rob publicly came clean and admitted that this event actually did occur back when he was a teenager, and he apologized to Mary in front of everyone in attendance.

Then, with a gleam in his eye, he turned to Mary and said, "But you know, Mary, you're still looking really good. Do you think that I might…?"

With that, Mary gave a broad smile and turned her buttock toward Rob. Rob reached out and grabbed her ass big time!

Everyone just roared at the antics of these two, and people were hysterically laughing! Who knows? Maybe someday we'll have a chance to see this footage as part of the *Revisited* show on DVD!

Day one of production was over—or at least I thought it was. Instead, I was approached and recruited by Paul Brownstein Productions to help work on the flashback clips that would be interspersed throughout the show. In reality, what this meant was that, after a long day at the soundstage, we would retreat to an editing studio to locate and edit clips from the original show. While it was exhausting to work into the night, it was just as exciting to be a part of, and contributor to, this show. This work also earned me a credit in the show's closing titles.

On day two, after all the years of phone conversations, I finally met Carl's assistant, Barbara Scher. I would never have been as successful as I have been with the newsletter without Barbara's help. Thank you Barbara for our wonderful association!

Day two was also the day that I seized one of my favorite keepsakes from *The Dick Van Dyke Show Revisited*—a photo of me coming through the front door of the Petrie Living room.

Media outlets were a constant presence on the set, with camera crews to shoot footage and interview the cast members about this very exceptional experience. And they were all there! CBS, Entertainment Tonight, Access Hollywood, and more!

Press photos were also taken, and promotional spots were filmed. One of the promo spots included one of Dick, Mary, Carl, and Rose Marie, where Dick was supposedly conducting the group in the singing of *The Dick Van Dyke Show* theme.

Dick directed as the four sang—"La la la la la la la la." He abruptly stopped them to point out that the words were not "La la la la la la la la." They were "Da da da da da da da da." What were they thinking?! It was very amusing and a cute bit. Unfortunately, this version never made it to the air although some of the footage was used a part of an edited promotion.

Day three of shooting afforded me the opportunity to have a leisurely lunch with Dick's publicist, Bob Palmer, at the CBS commissary. Bob has also been a key component in my success, facilitating numerous meetings with Dick and coordinating interviews and other press materials. And he's become a pretty good friend, too. Thanks Bob!

And I also had the chance to sit and visit with Ruth Engelhardt, the individual who has handled the affairs of Calvada Productions all of these "forty some" years that *The Dick Van Dyke Show* has been in existence. Ruth is a delightful and sweet lady, and it has been my sincere pleasure to get to know her and work with her.

My time on the set was just incredible. As the show completed its final take on the last day of shooting, Carl offered some closing remarks to the cast, crew, family, friends, and crowd of observers. Goodbyes were exchanged, and everyone began to dissipate. It had been a remarkable few days.

As I returned to the bleachers to collect my camera and my signed *Revisited* script, I recalled the words uttered to me by Carl Reiner when I met up with him on the set on the first day of shooting.

"I think you're more excited about this production than I am," said Carl, "and this is *my* show."

Carl was probably right. No, he was definitely right! This experience was truly a once-in-a-lifetime opportunity and one which I will never forget. It was also a historical event in the annals of classic television since no other show has ever returned to network TV so many years after its original network debut. That says a lot in itself!

What a tremendous thrill it was for me as a fan of the show to be able to be part of this project—at the invite of the man himself! My dream had been realized, thanks to Carl Reiner, forty years later!

# 17

## *The Final Chapter*

Yes, The Final Chapter—an apropos name, no?

When I began the newsletter in 1995, I was often asked by friends what I would do when I ran out of material to publish. My response? I told them I would have to deal with that problem when I encountered it.

The reality? I have never had to deal with such a dilemma. Over the course of the life of the publication, I have somehow always managed to have original and interesting material to share with fans.

As I look back over the past decade, I would assert that the newsletter's success is attributable to two major factors.

The first is the simple fact that I had something absolutely wonderful to write about. The fact that *The Dick Van Dyke Show* has endured for over forty years is due to the supreme quality of the writing, outstanding directing, and the stellar performances of the cast. The show has never been off the air since its original network run ended in 1966 and has most recently been discovered by a third generation of fans who are newly interested in learning about the lives of Rob, Laura, Ritchie, Buddy, Sally, and Mel—not to mention Millie and Jerry and the egomaniacal Alan Brady.

The second, and, undoubtedly, most significant factor that allowed the newsletter to fully realize its potential, has been the unwavering support and endorsement of my publication by *The Dick Van Dyke Show* cast and crew.

I am often reminded by associates as to the magnitude of what I have been able to accomplish with my publication. Not only have I been able to pay tribute to a wonderful show, I have also somehow managed to carve my own little niche in the show's history and be graciously welcomed into *The Dick Van Dyke Show* family.

It became evident to me as I sat on the set of *The Dick Van Dyke Show Revisited* that I was now a "member" of something very special. Carl had thought enough of my work to invite me and include me to join them during his production. What higher compliment could I be paid?

As I contemplated my involvement with the show, I came to the realization that the reason I was included was that I wasn't an "outsider" any more. I had earned the respect of those who were directly involved with the show and was now really an "insider."

Who could have possibly envisioned when I started the newsletter that I would have the opportunity to get to meet and come to know the cast so well, produce a documentary about the walnut episode, help in and contribute to the production of the show on DVD, attend the TV Land Awards and party with the cast, and ultimately have the "once in a lifetime" chance to contribute to and be part of *The Dick Van Dyke Show Revisited?*

The answer is…not me! This experience has been an extraordinary and absolutely amazing journey and one that I still have difficulty comprehending. How delighted I am to have been the one to perpetuate the myth of *The Dick Van Dyke Show*. The show is a jewel in the history of classic television and will continue to entertain countless generations of fans for years to come.

No particle of absorbitron will ever diminish my sense of humor nor cause me to lose my thumbs. To the contrary, I offer a huge "thumbs up" to the cast and crew of *The Dick Van Dyke Show*. While all of them are extremely talented individuals, more than anything, they are all wonderful people!

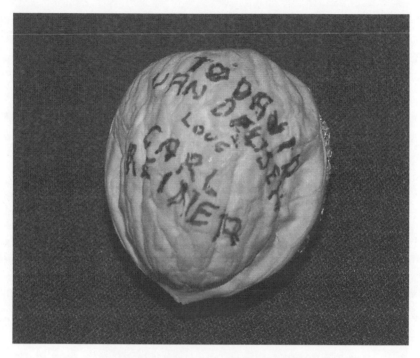

An autographed, absorbitron laden walnut
"To David Van Deusen, Love Carl Reiner"

# *About the Author*

## *David Van Deusen*

Recognized as the "Head Walnut" by Dick Van Dyke and "the other DVD" by Carl Reiner, David Van Deusen has been publishing *The Walnut Times, The Dick Van Dyke Show* newsletter, since 1995.

Besides Van Dyke and Reiner, Van Deusen has done interviews and established relationships with nearly every member of the cast and crew including Mary Tyler Moore, Rose Marie, Larry Mathews, Ann Guilbert, Bill Idelson, director John Rich, music man Earle Hagen, writer/producer Sam Denoff, film editor Bud Molin, and the now deceased Morey Amsterdam and Sheldon Leonard.

Over the past 10 years, Van Deusen has been acknowledged as an expert on the show, advising on various television specials about Dick Van Dyke and *The Dick Van Dyke Show* and providing photos and research materials to Image Entertainment and Paul Brownstein Productions as they moved forward to release the definitive collection of the five seasons of *The Dick Van Dyke Show* on DVD. He has also written and produced a documentary on the making of the famous "It May Look Like a Walnut" episode.

Van Deusen participated in the production of the Emmy nominated *Dick Van Dyke Show Revisited* special which aired to huge ratings on CBS in May 2004, assisting in the research and development of the flashback clip segments included in the program. He is currently consulting on the bonus footage under consideration for inclusion on the proposed DVD release of *The Dick Van Dyke Show Revisited*.

For more information about *The Walnut Times*, stop by the website for a visit at www.thewalnuttimes.com or mail to *The Walnut Times*, PO Box 622, Slingerlands, NY 12159.

978-0-595-37380-2
0-595-37380-1

Made in the USA